Praise for *Letters to the Earth*:

'By healing the Earth, we heal ourselves. By loving it, we love ourselves. And by telling its stories, we tell our own, and ensure that they will continue. All power to this amazing project'

JOANNE HARRIS

'A beautiful book calling for us to look after the place we call home ... Read it, then buy it for everyone you know'

Red Magazine

'The personal, the poetic, the dramatic, the salvo, the call to action; it's all here, in this timely anthology'

JINI REDDY, *The Ecologist*

'A wonderful little book'   JEROME FLYNN

'An extraordinary book. Reading it will remind you of our enduring connection to this planet we call home, and the urgency with which we need to respond to the climate crisis. The letters speak of how much we stand to lose if we fail to take action now. I encourage you to read them'

STEPHEN DALDRY, director of *Billy Elliot*

'*Letters to the Earth* is a compelling ode to the elemental and fundamental aspects of our planet ... a must-read for anyone who lives on earth'

BELLA LACK, conservationist and
Born Free Youth Ambassador

Letters
to the Earth

Writing to a Planet in Crisis

Introduction by Emma Thompson

WILLIAM
COLLINS

William Collins
An imprint of HarperCollins*Publishers*
1 London Bridge Street
London SE1 9GF

WilliamCollinsBooks.com

HarperCollins*Publishers*
1st Floor, Watermarque Building, Ringsend Road
Dublin 4, Ireland

First published in Great Britain in 2019 by William Collins
This William Collins paperback edition published in 2021

1

Printed and bound in Great Britain by
CPI Group (UK) Ltd, Croydon

Contents

Love

Loss

Emergence

Hope

Action

Introduction

All humans know somewhere deep – somewhere like our spinal cords, somewhere we are not used to communicating with – that our planet is suffering. We know at a cellular level and it is causing us huge distress. It's like being in a sci-fi story where we are under attack from the Martians – except in this story we are the Martians and there is no spaceship out there poised to save us from destruction. But let's remember that because we are the authors of the story we can also be the authors of what comes next.

So many of our inventions – miraculous at the time – gas, coal, planes, cars, smoking (I loved it) are now the agents of destruction. It's hard to let go of our addictions, so hard. But let go we must if we, and the greater web of life of which we are, after all, only a part, are to survive.

I wonder what the best way of helping us understand that is. The Intergovernmental Panel on Climate Change (IPCC) reports, the terrifying documentaries, the relentless roll-call of climate disasters spread fearfully essential knowledge and are vital, of course. It goes without saying that we must educate ourselves and see for ourselves what is taking place. But something else needs to happen if our fear and rage and frustration are to succeed in transforming our world.

These writings have pulled me back into focus.

I can remember now how many bees I used to see in parks and gardens in London and on the hills of Argyll. I can remember the variety of butterflies, their miraculous beauty, strength and fragility. I realise how little I now see them and how heartbroken it makes me. I miss them in the visceral way I miss members of my family long since dead.

We all need to plug into our love for our home, our planet, our earth. The astronauts describe it so well – those people with fiercely trained scientific minds who may not necessarily open themselves to poetic imagination (that might be too dangerous). They suddenly see the vulnerable beauty of our pale blue dot in the reaches of dark space. They feel huge love and empathy for it and, crucially, they feel deeply protective.

Art – in all its forms – can turn us all into astronauts. It can help us out of the prison of assumption and the caverns of ignorance into the atmosphere of clarity and hope. The temptation to panic is very great but panic will always prevent useful action. I panic regularly about the planet and then I will often turn to small, everyday actions. One of them is to sit and contemplate the beauty of nature – to go to a park and read and look up every so often at the sky or at a tree and remind myself that while we are here, we can care for our home.

Or I can transform my panic by joining larger actions – like the XR protest at Oxford Circus which was so memorable and full of love. Standing on the pink boat reading Jackie Morris's exquisite, anguished lament to the swallow was an extraordinary experience. I looked out over so many faces – some people, overwhelmed with grief, wept openly. The police came and stood around us but the atmosphere was peculiarly peaceful. Public moments of sharing – particularly the sharing of art – change the spaces and alter the atmosphere. This can give us vital strength. We must engage in these acts because – make no mistake – the ruling powers will not do enough to alter the course of this terrifying history. We are on our own and together we will have to make them.

My vision is sometimes blurred by the horror of the millions of deaths our fossil fuel habits have caused and by the certain knowledge that all of this will continue to get worse until it gets better – because so much of what we have done is irreversible.

But in the end, hopelessness serves no purpose. Fighting for everything climate change reversal represents, from the essential bee to global social justice, will never offer anything but active hope.

We must combine the determined and unstoppable organisation of our best instincts with the vision of astronauts.

The wave of change is here. The generation below mine is different. I feel it and I read it in these letters. They know we have failed them and instead of wasting time blaming us or even trying to punish us they simply act. The young do not mind change as much as the old.

They are our best hope and listening to them always makes me feel powerful once again. Plugging into that energy will recharge even the most tired of batteries.

Read this book and pass it on. Hand on your passion for the planet to the next person and never, ever give in. Convert your rage to action and your grief to love. I think the planet feels us as we do this. Perhaps it will even help us.

Emma

Dear Reader,

Just under two years ago a small group of women came together around a kitchen table to talk. We had been profoundly shaken by the increasingly dire reports of climate and ecological collapse, but inspired by the work of Extinction Rebellion and the Youth Strikers in bringing that news to the forefront of the public conversation. In our working lives we are theatre-makers and writers; we felt strongly that we wanted to find a way to facilitate a creative response to these times of emergency. For so long – too long – our professions had been eerily silent about this greatest of subjects. Why? Was this a failure of nerve? Of imagination?

We knew Extinction Rebellion was planning a huge, disruptive action in the streets of London, and we began to imagine a creative campaign that might sit alongside and speak to that moment. As we talked and shared ideas, we sensed that this was a chance to hear from those who sit outside the usual theatrical and publishing circles, to take the pulse of the country in these times of growing anxiety and realisation.

From that initial conversation others were born; we met people, listened, and soon the idea of a *Letter to the Earth* emerged, a callout to the public to write a letter in response to the climate and ecological emergency. The letter could be to or from the earth, future or past generations, those who hold positions of power and influence, or other species. It was an open invitation to anyone who wished to take part. We also invited venues to come on board and host a reading of the letters.

An email account was created and on a cold February morning the callout went live. We waited, a little nervously. The inbox was quiet. Then one letter arrived, and another, then our first batch of schoolchildren's letters, twenty or more young people responding to the call. The letters were moving, disturbing, vital. The inbox kept filling: pictures drawn by seven-year-olds, letters from teenagers, nurses, great-grandparents. Letters were coming in from all around the world, from published poets and from people who had never put pen to paper before. In reading through them, there were many occasions when one or other of us was caught short, moved to tears on public transport, or by the electric rise of the hairs on your arm when you know you are in the presence of something great, a truly remarkable piece of writing. This great unsayable thing, this anxiety, this fear, this love, was finding expression in so many voices. Their cumulative power was overwhelming.

Meanwhile, venue after venue was signing up: a Ukrainian Club in Huddersfield, a Conservative Club in Paddington, a pub in Kent, leading theatres up and down the country: the Royal Court, the National Theatre of Wales, Shakespeare's Globe, and venues around the world, from Alabama to South Africa to Zambia. By the time submissions closed we had almost a thousand letters in our keeping, an astonishing gift. We believe it to be the largest creative response to these times of crisis the world has yet seen. On Friday 12 April, a day of global youth strike, the letters were read at fifty-two venues worldwide. During the International Spring Rebellion, in which Extinction Rebellion occupied five sites in central London for two weeks, the letters were read from every stage. From the truck in the centre of Marble Arch, from a single microphone in front of seated lines of people willingly putting themselves up for arrest on Waterloo Bridge, from the grass in the middle of Parliament Square, and, perhaps most memorably, from the top of Berta Cáceres, the now iconic pink boat, when youth strikers and performers came together on the XR 'Day of Love'.

And now this collection: it was not easy to choose from such a rich variety of voices, and the book could easily have been twice as long, but the following selection feels both challenging and vital. We have gathered the letters into five headings: Love, Loss, Emergence, Hope, Action. The headings are not prescriptive, though they may serve as a prescription: if you feel despair, turn to Hope; if you feel loss, you may find comfort in voices who feel as you do; or you may need to read poems that immerse you in love for this home we all share.

We encourage you, too, to read the book from start to finish, but if you do so you will see that this is not a simple journey from Love to Action: love also contains fear and anger, hope contains despair. This is not comfortable reading. It is not comfortable to read the words of teenagers who fear they will have no future, of children begging for change. Of adults horrified by the world they are complicit in creating. Of mothers who despair for their young. Of those stricken by grief at the daily, catastrophic loss of the living world they hold so dear.

Some of the boldest voices speaking to us through this collection are those from the Global South, in countries where ecological and climate catastrophe are a lived reality. Daniela Torres Perez challenges us not to turn a blind eye to the suffering of her home country Peru: 'a place where the people with the least money are the ones that suffer most'. As climate breakdown arrives on the doorstep of those living in the north, it is important to remember this wider reality, one in which people of colour and people living in poverty have long been disproportionately affected by ecological breakdown. Renato Redentor Constantino, writing from the Philippines, invites us to imagine 'an island travelling south, a landscape on the move where compassion is the currency, and solidarity the only debt people owe each other.' To speak of climate justice is to recognise its inextricable connection to racial and social justice. We cannot have one without the other.

As the climate and ecological emergency continues to unfold, letters continue to be written. The global pandemic has reminded us of our connectedness, of our reliance upon each other, and how swiftly a fragile ecosystem can be thrown into chaos. In a new letter, the Nigerian poet Ben Okri reflects on the events of the past year and writes that we are at the 'beginning of an age of catastrophes', and that we must listen to the earth's 'silent wisdom' in order to live again. This coming decade will be testing and transformative; requiring a leap of imagination and tremendous courage from us all.

There are no easy answers contained within these pages, no clear paths out of the maze in which we find ourselves, but there is courage here and there is hope, hope that – in the words of Joanna Macy – is active, that calls us to action. There is love that echoes and speaks back to loss. Voices that dare to imagine a more beautiful, equitable, generous way of being with ourselves, each other and all those who share this living, interdependent, planet that we call home.

Write a Letter; be part of the story.

With love, and hope,
Anna Hope, Jo McInnes, Kay Michael, Grace Pengelly
February 2021

In the Beginning

Dear Author of Genesis,

I know it's pointless to begin like this, because you lived about three thousand years ago and are no longer around to answer my questions, but I think you would appreciate what I am trying to do in this letter, so I'll carry on. You were a creative writer, an artist, and writers play around with words in ways that non-writers don't always understand. It is the way you have been misunderstood that bothers me. In fact, not understanding you has brought the world you wrote about so lovingly to a moment of great danger, a danger I want to tell you about.

You started with these words: '*In the beginning* God created the heavens and the earth.' And that's how your book got its name, Genesis, *Beginning*. Then you went on to craft a great poem describing how God made everything in six days and rested on the seventh. That's where the trouble started. I wish you had added a little note inviting your readers to take you seriously but not literally. In fact, I wish you had written a prologue on the art of reading. I wish you had reminded us that you were an artist responding imaginatively to the wonder of the universe, not a reporter taking notes on something happening in real time. But that's how some people started to read you. Not as a glorious fiction that prompted their wonder, but as an accurate news report of a tumultuous week about six thousand years ago. You won't believe this, but there are people alive in my time who insist on reading you that way. We could dismiss them all as endearing eccentrics, if it weren't for something else they get wrong, something they again take *literally* – and this time it's had consequences, very serious consequences.

On the sixth or last 'day' of your narrative, God creates all the living creatures on earth, the grand climax being the emergence of humanity, God's special favourite.

> 'So God created man in his own image, in the image
> of God he created him; male and female he created
> them.'

Then come the fateful instructions to these human beings about how they are supposed to live:

> 'And God blessed them, and God said to them, Be
> fruitful and multiply, and fill the earth, and subdue it:
> and have dominion over the fish of the sea, and over the
> birds of the air, and over every living thing that moves
> upon the earth.'

I want to pause for a moment to reflect on what you thought you were doing when these words came to you. Great writers don't tell us *about* something. Their writing *becomes* the thing itself. Is that what you were doing here? Were you writing with a premonitory sorrow over the meaning of these words? In a single sentence you captured humanity's arrogance, its belief that it owned or had *dominion* over the earth, and could do anything it liked with it. And that's what we have done. The planet is marked with the smudge and ugliness of our abuse of it. It is littered with the debris of our greed.

To be fair to us – or to some of us – we have begun to realise what we have done to the planet in our arrogance, and we are trying to make amends. We have started cleaning up the rivers we polluted. We are trying to purify the air over our cities we have saturated with toxic particles. We are even beginning to worry about the effect of losing the species we have rendered extinct. But now some of us are beginning to wonder if it might all be too little too late. A bit like deciding to spring-clean a house on the edge of a cliff that's about to plunge into the sea because of coastal erosion. It's the earth, our home, that's now on the edge of that cliff. All because we didn't know how to read what you had written. Because we read your words not as a warning, not as a fable that required interpretation, but as an instruction manual to be followed to the letter. Look where it's got us.

It gets worse. There are literalists out there who believe this is what God actually wants. And because they don't know how to read, they've come up with a god who hates the world so much he is coming soon to destroy it and everything in it. Except them, of course. They'll be saved as the planet combusts. That's why they welcome its extinction. 'Use it before you lose it, the end is nigh,' they yell, believing their divinely chartered spaceship is standing by to take them to safety. How could I sum up their attitude for you, dear author of Genesis? 'Fuck the planet, *we're* gonna be OK,' is probably as close as I can get.

So I hope you understand now why I am writing to you. It's not that I wish you'd been a bit more careful in how you wrote your parable. It's just that I wish you'd made it clearer what you were doing when you started composing your great fiction. On the other hand, it's hardly your fault there are so many humans who completely lack imagination. But why do so many of them claim to be religious? Don't they understand that religion is the oldest art? And that its stories are to be read seriously, but never literally? Enough already.

The good news is that young people everywhere are rebelling against humanity's God-given right to destroy the earth, their home. *Their* religion is love of the little blue planet that bore them and sustains them. And they are fighting hard to save it. You'd admire them. You'd want to write something to help them. Or maybe you would just point to something another writer from your own family of artists would say hundreds of years later. His name was Isaiah and these are his words:

> 'The wolf shall dwell with the lamb, and the leopard
> shall lie down with the kid, and the calf and the lion
> and the fatling together, *and a little child shall lead them.*'

And you know what, old friend? I'm tempted to read that poem literally!

Richard Holloway

Love

Earth

The earth's name is unique. We need to keep it.

> **E** = Energetic
> **A** = Amazing
> **R** = Respectful
> **T** = Trusty
> **H** = Happy

The letters of the EARTH are what keeps us alive, without it we will be extinct.

Please forgive us for our mistakes.

It's up to us to support the earth.

Emily Trenouth-Wood, 11

In the Climbing Hydrangea of my Neighbour's Fence

I got up this morning and took my mug of tea to the open window. I could hear the sound of blackbirds and blue tits on the grassy bank and in the hawthorn trees that edge the field behind my garden. I stood and felt the warm sun on my skin and watched as they flew: blue, black, brown, grey, yellow, red, with straw and moss in their beaks for lining their nests.

There was a little nest, exposed by the winter, in the climbing hydrangea on my neighbour's fence – the separation that was required between our spaces. It was perfect, nestled against the creosoted panels – once proud trees – and the gardener's wire that holds the sprawling plant upright. I imagined the mother there with her babies, safe and secure behind a wall of lush green vegetation. Shielded from the prying eyes of next door's ginger tomcat.

The sun went behind a scudding spring cloud and I watched as a pair of rooks walked along the top of the wall below the bird feeder, surveying the scene, pretending to each other that they hadn't found a tasty worm or juicy seed. My eye travelled down towards the newly planted pond, a swish and a splash and the smooth newt had disappeared back below the surface of the green-tinged water. The plants are beginning to grow up around it – the ragged robin and clary sage, the water plantain and flowering rush in their first spurt of spring. I opened the door and stepped outside into my wildlife haven and stood beside the pond. I am as still as the green-black pool.

My mind was empty of the day, empty of children and mortgages, cars and cleaning, housework, ironing, shopping, meetings and things to be done, bought and consumed. A collared dove, soft grey and heavy, landed on a hawthorn bough and it bowed under the bird's weight. A second joined it and I closed my eyes to listen to the soft cooing they made to one another as they walked up and down the branches, their heads bobbing as they searched for insects. I am a quiet intruder in their busy lives.

My patio and flower beds, the concrete and paving stones, houses, high-rises, office blocks and motorways, reservoirs and dams seem to me, to us, to take precedence as we order and build nature out of existence. The ancient forests of Britain, Amazonia, Romania, Borneo, Ghana, the eastern United States, Mexico and Australia have been razed to the ground. I have destroyed half of all the trees on earth. I have killed my brothers and sisters for decking and picture frames, warmth and convenience.

I opened my eyes and looked up to the vast blue expanse of sky, swirled with wispy clouds and heard the high-pitched pewee-pewee of a red kite high above, circling. Two more appeared and then suddenly there were eight or ten red kites, their tails dipping and turning as they swooped in great arcs, riding thermals, thriving and free. I drained my mug of tea, now gone cold, and headed back inside, my heart filled, my mind clear as I sat down at my desk to write a letter to the earth.

Justine Railton

Dear Mr Walnut Tree

Dear Mr Walnut Tree,

I would like to apologise on the behalf of mankind for ruining your beautiful earth. I would also like to thank you for holding strong and even managing to hold my weight, year after year. Thank you for being such an easy-to-climb tree, and thank you for being there whenever I have needed you. I would also like to say sorry on the behalf of my dad for leaning the old fence on your trunk. I hope you don't mind me swinging on you all the time.

I'm sorry for carving my initials at the very top of you with my penknife. I shan't do it again, I promise.

Just a quick question – were you planted or did you just grow naturally? If you were planted, when was it? And who did it?

I'm sorry for not maintaining a clean and tidy space around you on the floor of the garden. And the most utterly sincere apology that I would like to make to you today is that I'm truly sorry for letting Mum pay that stupid old man to come along and chop your head off last year.

I hope you enjoy your current position in the garden, and if you don't, please feel very free to ask if you would like to be moved.

Thank you for not dying yet even though you live next to two apple trees that I'm not even sure are alive. Let's just call them the 'apple producing zombie trees'.

To conclude I would like to say don't die, carry on living bold and strong for as long as you possibly can.

YOURS SINCERELY YOUR CLIMBER,
Benedict C. Winter, 12

Milk

You gave me milk when I arrived, sweet and warm. And slowly colours came; they had no names, not then, and the sounds no source. I had no hands, no feet. I was just breath slowly folding into skin and there was no soil, no rain, not a leaf or a shell.

At four years old you gave me fields and stars waiting; they are still waiting. Then streams and banks thick with grass began to appear, a path lined with daffodils, wet sand and gulls calling from within the light coming off the sea baptising everything. You hid so many jewels: blue eggs in lined nests, sparkling feathers, pink and yellow shells, small silver fishes. And at night silent and moving closer now, wolves and pulling waters.

You didn't show me the dawn and the dusk until I was able to be still, until I was able to open these doors by myself. To know them as beginnings and endings. We were always part of each other. I am salts and water as is every leaf, every lion, every hill. And I am every river, every flower, every wave, every stone and they are me, the hunted and the hunter.

Now I can see you shining, glistening, moving through space, around the star holding your precious cargo of whales, goldcrests, petals. Yes, your cargo of dreams, of love distilling every bitter seed. Brushed with clouds.

It is my hope that love will prevail – that we will prevail through loving, through knowing every seed and star is love. That in time I will hold you as you hold me. That we will know the end of isolation and the beckoning of the reality of interdependence. That this is balance which is wisdom, look at the route the river takes. The branches leaning into the light.

I give you thanks. For the dew, for the sound of leaves, for the way water moves light, for birdsong, for the deserts, for hunger. For the cup of desire.

I have yet to learn that looking after myself begins with loving you, that we are husband and wife, that I sleep in your arms and drink your milk.

And now growing older you show me the symmetry of leaves, how death takes hold and how deep your scent is sweet in spring.

Peter Owen Jones

All the Trees

This week all the trees in my street are blossoming
And the world turns around again.
But we are eleven years, six months and counting
To hold on to what we have.

Tilly Lunken

But the Greatest of These Is Love

It's finally happening. We're finally talking about climate change. It's messy, but it's happening. To be honest, we don't really have the language, and that's largely because we don't know how to feel about it.

For decades, the dominant narrative has been that we should feel guilt. Then, there's the dual narrative that calls for hope. Others have called for fear, or panic. I myself am on the record calling for anger.

But I don't always feel angry, to tell the truth. In fact, sometimes I'm hopeful, sometimes I'm scared. Sometimes I'm overwhelmed, and sometimes I'm downright stubborn. (My mama would tell you that's pretty much all the time.)

That's because none of those emotions really get to the heart of what I truly feel. None of them are big enough. If I'm honest with myself, what I truly feel is ... love.

Hear me out.

I don't mean any simple, sappy kind of love. I don't mean anything cute or tame. I mean living, breathing, heart-beating love. Wild love. This love is not a noun, she is an action verb. She can shoot stars into the sky. She can spark a movement. She can sustain a revolution.

I love this beautiful, mysterious, complicated planet we get to call home. The planet who had the audacity to burst with life, from her boreal crown to her icy toes at the South Pole. I love her caves and her valleys and her rivers and her oceans. I love the majesty of larger-than-life elephants and whales and rhinos and lions. I love the elegance and enigma of all the different kinds of bats – even the ones that eat *other bats*! I love the unapologetic sass of butterflies and hummingbirds and coral reefs and the tear-jerking aroma of flowers that bloom below the equator.

I love that night-time symphony on steamy southern nights when the frogs croak and the crickets sing and the owls hunt. I love the taste of watermelon and blackberries in the summer – the way that they ooze down the side of my face when they've reached perfect ripeness. I love the delicate feel of honeysuckle petals and the warm, grainy earth and dewy grass on my bare feet.

I love sitting on my mama's back porch in Mississippi to watch 'God do his work' in the form of late summer thunderstorms underneath a thick blanket of humidity. I love the late summer haze when all the colours come to life and seem to throb.

And I love my mama. I love my family. I love my niece and nephew and I love that it doesn't matter that their parents are actually my cousins and not my siblings. I love my Aunt Joyce's laugh and my cousin Candice's freckles and my Aunt Karen's voice.

I love – dare I say it? – myself. And some days it's easier to do that than others. Sometimes it feels impossible, but it's a work in progress and I'm working on it, OK?

A love like this doesn't live in your heart. She's too big for that. She's in your blood, your bones. She's in your DNA. The places where people think racism is. She envelops you with an impenetrable armour.

When you love something, or someone, that much, of course you're frightened when you see her under attack, and of course you're furious at anyone or anything that would dare to harm her.

I am furious that my mother is in more and more danger every hurricane season. And I am terrified at the thought of living through my old age, when my body aches the way my mother's does now, in an unpredictable environment with disaster at every turn. What happens when my knees don't have enough spring left in them to run from a wildfire? What happens when I've lost it all in a flood, but I'm too old to work again?

But this love is strong enough to break through the terror. She is hot enough to burn through anger and turn into fury. She can shake you out of your despair and propel you to the front of the battlefield.

It's a love that can also – even in the teeth of these most insurmountable odds – give me hope. If I'm brave enough to accept it. I've seen her looking back at me in the eyes of some of the bravest climate justice warriors I have ever met, and I can feel that tickling tingle of 'maybe, just maybe, we'll be okay'.

A love like that doesn't seek peace, or even vengeance. She seeks justice. And she's strong enough, ferocious enough, brave enough to burn this bitch to the ground.

Mary Annaïse Heglar

Help Me Catch Our World

Dear Planet Earth,

I am sorry we have misused you, messed you up, and physically abused you.

Now we are pleading for forgiveness, although we have done nothing to stop it, we just brought it upon ourselves.

It's like watching a paper fall, and instead of catching it you watch it drop to the floor.

It's like watching a child drown, and instead of saving him, you slowly watch him sink, sink slowly to the ground.

Because planet earth, we had the chance to catch you. We had the chance to save you.

Though people chose to ignore you. They chose to look away and say, 'that's not my problem to face.'

I'm sorry that when you stumbled and fell, we didn't kiss your bruise better: we didn't place a plaster over your cut: we didn't even blow it better, we just left it, untouched. I'm sorry that we paid more attention to our problems, than we did yours. For we forgot that you, planet earth, are the reason we breathe and live, and us humans let that message pass our minds, way too quickly.

And for that I am truly sorry.

Help me correct our mistake.

Help me catch our world: *save our planet*.

Jenny Ngugi, 13

Letter to the Worms

A little girl about seven years old, lying on stubby brown August grass in a London back garden. Using the pale inner core of a stem of grass as her quill and a flat green blade of it as her papyrus, she writes intently and invisibly. When the letter is done, she folds it into a tiny parcel and drops it into a hole in the ground. She is writing to the worms.

Her postbox is unnaturally circular, its ridge barely breaking the surface of the tiny lawn, but showing as a greener ring where the rain is slower to drain away. It is the air-vent of the bomb shelter dug into this suburban garden during the Second World War, for the benefit of the local residents. Now it is a portal to a subterranean universe where, via these green deliveries, the child's secrets may be unburdened. Afterwards, if she lies on the ground and listens carefully, she feels a sort of comfort coming back to her, though not in actual words. Neighbours stare from above. She ignores them.

It is too hot and dry for gardening and the ground is hard. This means that the worms are safe because when it's wet, she has seen them writhing and racing as the metal fork lifts them to the light. Sometimes the spade cuts them in half, but both pieces continue to writhe, contorting with agony – that much is clear. She marvels at the news worms can regrow themselves after what looks like certain death. Worms must be magical like Jesus, or else Jesus is a kind of worm. She is told never ever to say this again.

At school, she ponders the origin of the hard grey-pink slices on her plate, coated in gluey brown gravy. 'Eat your roast,' is all the dinner lady will say, so she sits there chewing away, a feeling of disgust filling her mouth as finally the fibres grow mushy. She cannot swallow it, so surreptitiously she transfers bite after bite under the table, onto a little ledge that seems purpose-built for concealment. Then she goes out to play, until there is uproar from the dinner ladies clearing the hall. The whole school is called back to their exact dining places, and the culprit is discovered and rebuked for wasting good beef. When in distress and shame she says she does not want to eat cows, her parents are called to the school, where they are asked if it is for religious reasons (it is not). There then follows a discussion of her strangeness and lack of friends. The little girl has no explanation, but listens and can only silently agree with what they say. Fortunately it is the end of term.

Under the hot sun, the inside of the chimney vent is still cool. Its black depths smell mysterious and cavelike, but there is no echo. She wishes that the whole garden would fall down into the earth, dropping past the Second World War and down to the Romans, who, she has heard on the radio, used potato leaves to commit suicide. These are close to hand, which feels like some sort of sign.

She writes again to the worms in her best green calligraphy, informing them of her loneliness and plan to die. She writes that when they or their families come across her body, she will be pleased to meet them and learn from them, for instance, how they swim through soil, eat the earth, and survive death by spade. She says she knows they are also strong and can be very fast, because she has seen them emerge after rain, making dangerous and mysterious journeys across pavements. So they are also brave.

She posts her last letter, picks a good handful of potato leaves, and lies down on the ground to listen for a response. After that, she will go to her room and eat them. But the worms have no comment. It is as if they have gone away, because there is a new and strange feeling of disconnection with the underworld. The idea comes to her that perhaps they have gone somewhere else; perhaps even worms can enjoy summer holidays, just not her. Perhaps they have travelled to investigate buried treasure – maybe a Roman hoard. Beneath the earth, they might be completely free.

She considers the idea of hidden treasure. It might be close by. She notices the ants clearing out sand from their holes, then bigger ants with white wings emerge, and take to the sky. There is a trembling feeling in the air, and clouds at last. She transfers her attention to the ants. There is a lot to observe and she forgets the leaves. That night there is a huge angry outburst in the sky. It is very pleasing.

Laline Paull

Insects

To the Earth,

For many years I had been fortunate to work with insects. They are some of the most beautiful creatures on earth. They are often so tiny that nature hides them. But I learned about the smallest of them through the lens of a microscope. I marvel that they can be so beautiful and yet so few people get to see them! What a privilege it was to work with them – years that felt more like playing than working ...

And what strange a process that happened here on earth – the evolution of such diversity! And so extraordinarily intricate!

How is it then that we are letting these incredible life forms down? Selfishly for thousands of years we humans only saw our own importance and mastery. Now we have to wake up and at last see *their* importance and realise that their lives are also ours – humans cannot live without this diversity in nature.

Ottilie Neser

I Love You, Earth

I love you, earth, you are beautiful
I love the way you are
I know I never said it to you
But I wanna say it now

I love you, I love you
I love you, earth
I love you, I love you
I love you now

I love you, earth, you are beautiful
I love the way you shine
I love your valleys, I love your mornings
In fact I love you everyday

I know I never said it to you
Why I'd never know
Over blue mountains, over green fields
I wanna scream about it now

I love you, I love you
I love you, earth
I love you, I love you
I love you now

You are our meeting point of infinity
You are our turning point in eternity

I love you, I love you
(I love you, I love you)
I love you, earth
I love you, I love you
(I love you, I love you)
I love you now
I love you, I love you
(I love you, I love you)
I love you, earth
I love you, I love you
(I love you, I love you)
I love you now

Yoko Ono

Dear Earth,

Listen, I'm sorry for all the pain I have brought upon you, I have given you temperatures, I have given you colds that have caused you to sneeze hurricanes in defense.
Yes we are thoughtless; yes we are foolish.
But a large portion of our race are aware that we must cure your illness. Our potions and constructions are killing your worker bees, and this is killing us, So we must help you to heal ourselves, so please have mercy! you have nurtured and looked after us, now it is our turn.

Yours Sincerely,

Kaylen Van Veldhoven

39

Stories of You and I

1.

My fingertips pushed through the mossy earth, into the
    damp soil, wriggling deeper.
The texture of the roots between my fingers, some thick and
    almost rubbery, others
delicate and fine, webs, rhizomes.
The clay, the silt, the sand, the worm casts crumbled in my
    hands.
All day I carried the smell of fresh earth on my fingers.
Oh how much I wanted to push down right into you, my
    love, to be consumed by you.
To feel myself sink into your depths, my dear, to take shelter
    in your underworld.

The majesty of the mountains revealed themselves as I
    ascended.
Tremendous expanses of daunting beauty.
Above, vultures circled.
Up here, where the air is thin, on the rocky outcrops, awe
    belongs to you alone, my love.
The insects, the wildflowers, the so many ladybirds, the
    highland meadows thronged with life.
My heart ached.
Oh to curl up here, my dear, and listen to the wildlife
    creeping out after dark.

To contemplate the stars as the temperature plummets and
    my nose drips with the biting cold.

I sat by the fire.
Pine cones glowed orange, the needles hissed and spat, sap
    oozed from a green wood
branch and the wood from the ash tree burned slow and hot.
In the flickering light of the dancing flame, silence and
    conversation, all welcome by the crackling fire.

The fluidity, the creativity, the passion, it was all there, my
    love.
The fire radiated through me and I could taste the sweat and
    smoke on my lips.
Oh to be so enthralled by you, my dear.
To be pulled so close my cheeks burned red.

The skin on the back of my neck tingled with the ice-cold
    water of the river.
I looked down at my legs, glistening and distorted, my feet
    wrapped over a smooth
pebble, holding fast against the rushing water.
The little fish, the tadpoles, the river-weed tangled up with
    my feet, my skin flushed pink.
I went numb, for a bit, my love.
The sound of the flowing water lulled me, I spoke quietly to
    myself.
I bent down, submerged my face, the water lapping against
    my lips.

Oh how it is to feel your energy in the water, my dear.
To feel it in my scalp, shivering down my body.

2.

Now, I thank you, my love, for walking this walk with me.
You have been the finest companion.
You have walked me through such happiness and joy, such
    sadness and confusion.
With you it has all been welcome. It has all been all
    right.

And now, I question, what sort of companion was I?
For all that I celebrated you and revelled in your wonder, I
    see now that I did not honour
you, nor hold you in true reverence.
I was here, you were there, and so I walked with you
    sometimes, and then went elsewhere.
I admired you from afar.

And from that comfortable distance, I could not *feel* how I
    too was caught up in
exploiting you, diminishing you.
I made you an object, myself a subject.
We stood apart.
You, and I.

And now, I wonder, who has suffered most, from this story of
    you, and I?
Because you, my love, were never 'nature'.

42

And I ...
I was never anything else.

3.

Now, in the silence, I stretch my fingers wide and rest my
    hands on my belly.
I breathe deep and slow.
No clenched fists, an open heart, tender, no fear in fragility.
My feet stand firm, my roots.
My skin burns.
Here, this is the unbearably perfect.

Now, one.
These scars are ours.
Now, into the wilderness, into the hostile world that has
    fought, so long, to silence our truth.
Into the city.
Now, with all our beauty, all our grief, all our shame, all our
    pain.
For all that we hold dear, for all that we love, for all that *we
    are*.
Now, it's time we walk as one.

Sally Jane Hole

Extinction Redemption

As a teen, I wore a T-shirt quoting Chief Seattle. 'The Earth is our mother,' it said. 'Man did not weave the web of life; he is merely a strand in it. Whatever he does to the web, he does to himself.' Looking back, I can see how I turned away from the depth and clarity of that insight. I listened to other stories of my time – stories so commonplace that I did not even see them as stories.

I listened to the story that if I wasn't pragmatic I would come to regret my choices. I worried that if I chose to live according to my truth then I might become poor or marginalised, and come to see such truth as a youthful naivety. I worried that I'd be too radical and so have no significant impact. These were powerful stories that carried me into a well-meaning, hard-working career.

Now looking back at these early choices, I can see that beneath it all there was something more primal. I was scared I'd lose someone that I loved. Not someone specific, but someone I hadn't even met yet. Someone that I thought I'd need to impress: with status, charisma, confidence, wealth, style and skills. Such things would need to be worked for, within our dominant culture and economy. I was lying to myself and to others because I was scared that I wouldn't be able to belong on my own terms.

Those insecurities meant I pushed away the implications of knowing that our society is based on a lie of the separation between humans, nature and spirit. For decades I compromised with that greatest of lies, and in so doing I was complicit with the ongoing destruction and oppression of you.

It took the terrifying data on climate change to shake me out of those delusions. Awakening to the likely collapse of society triggered a collapse in my sense of self-worth. My stomach churned and heaved with the horror of realising how much I'd been imprisoned by fear. Falling to my hands and knees, my forehead on the soil, I cried and asked you, 'Please forgive me.'

Your response was immediate.

I began to sense that because you are one life, you have no issue with death. We may feel guilt about destruction, yet the thousands of species going extinct are not a suffering for you. In that, perhaps I may find redemption from this pain.

'We are part of the earth and it is part of us,' wrote Chief Seattle. I am an aspect of you, a potentiality of you. As you produced me and everything that we are, when I experience that unity, I know we are all forgiven.

Thank you. As awareness of our climate emergency grows, you have begun to provide us with a global near-death experience. We can wake up to our mortality and our fear of it. Some of us will come to see the stories built upon that fear over the past millennia. With climate chaos, you invite us to return to you. You offer us an extinction redemption.

I'm sorry. Please forgive me. Thank you. I love you.

Jem Bendell

A Break Up Poem

this is not a love letter to earth
its a break up poem to the atmospheric protection of the
 ozone layer
to that last defence we say see you later
nice knowing you
and like a bitter ex
we take our last breath and turn red
refuse to be the first to blink
then purple
im not losing first you think
then grey
then relapse

drunk texts in the middle of the night
hey sunrise
im just writing to say i miss the look in your eyes when you
 first wake up
i cant remember it now
all i think of is fog
or smog
or rain
and how much it hurts to be caught in your gaze

that burn peels my skin for days
mirrors
the kind of ache that sits underneath

you always wanted the best for me
so for you i started turning off the tap when im brushing my
    teeth
it wont bring you back but it keeps my conscience clear
but when theres no running water
its much harder to hide my tears

what i loved the most about you
was that you were never mine
not really
all that we discovered was made by you for us to find
you gave us life
made human kind
then we took too much
from you we mined
your heart
we stole your treasure
killed your children
distorted your weather
we thought we could not only control but we could sell your
    power
and now we face our final hour
but you, the earth, will carry on
after we are dead and gone

you built yourself to survive
and withstand far more than the test of time
so some monsters with machines that are powered by your
    most profitable child

are no match for you
because you are her
mother earth
the start the end
so undefined

lots of love
until next time

Niamh McCarthy

We Don't Shop at Waitrose

To my Baby Nephew Max,

When I was little, 2019 sounded like a year so far in the future that we'd never actually get there. But here we are – and so soon! When you're my age it'll be 2050, the middle of the century. Do you imagine that there'll be flying cars and we'll be living on the moon? I really want that to be your future, one of love and adventures, and I am sure it will be; human beings are resilient and magnificent animals that are capable of so much wonderfulness. But it will be harder for you than it was for me.

I don't want to scare you – but I'm scared. Scared that we've hurt the planet we all live on.

I hope you're angry at us, I hope you resent us for not doing enough, that we made an enemy of your future.

No, I don't want you to feel that, I want you to think we were stupid and idiotic, from the viewpoint of a more advanced age, like how we laugh at people from the Middle Ages for thinking the earth was flat (and I hope your conspiracy-mad dad doesn't still think it's flat by 2050 but there's no guarantee).

It might not count for much, but I want you to know that I care about what's happening to the planet. I feel like we are stuck inside the jaws of a big horrible monster whose spiky teeth are like the bars of a prison. I don't know how we get out, but I'm trying to help so it's not as bad for you.

Others can't face it, or feel powerless to protest, or actually think it's a fight we're made to feel guilty about. That guilt is because we are not rich, Max, we don't live in posh houses, we don't speak proper and we certainly don't shop at Waitrose. It's called being working class, but that's a vague term; what I mean is that our mums and dads work all day to make sure we have food and clothes and telly but that's it, and that's all day and every day for those basic needs. The ones 'fighting' and telling our mums and dads off for not fighting, a lot of them have lived in posh houses and have been on lots of holidays. I'm being a bit silly, they're normal people too, they can't help that they have had the accident of luxury and private healthcare because their great-great-great-great-great-great-grandparents owned all the land.

Sorry, your uncle is on a soapbox, you don't need to know this bit, but it gets on my tits.

But seriously (and it's pointless to blame these hundred-odd big businesses for all this), it's always people like me and your mum and dad who are called on to sort this stuff out, while Lord Snootington gets all huffy at us for not having helped sooner!

The Prime Minister in 2050 will also be begging us chimney-sweep-type people to sort all this out and do our bit, like your great-granddad did in the Second World War, but he and his kin were clever and said they'd only fight if they got to stand shoulder to shoulder with the snooty lot and get things like clean water and beds after they fought off a monster as bad as the planet-eating beast whose jaws we are now stuck in.

I wish I was your dad rather than your gay uncle who lives in Edinburgh and never gets to see you, so I could really tell you about how we should love one another and that love for our fellow humans is so important. I'm scared that the monsters like those your great-granddad fought will soon spring up everywhere and say that mummies, daddies, brothers, sisters and babies aren't allowed to live anywhere because their homes have been ruined by the planet getting too hot. They'll want to get rid of them, but we've got to stand up for those people!

The Norms would find this preachy, and under any other circumstances I'd be bright red with embarrassment that I'm even writing such things, but I love you, I love the planet and I love humanity and I want to have hope that we'll survive what we've done to it. We have to act on it, we have to talk about it, we have to protest; we have to. I don't know what else to say, other than I'm off to try to help.

All my love,
Your Uncle Simon

Be Kind

I push it on to the next
Sending them complex
Trying to impress
I'm angry at myself
Angry at people for not loving
Does that make me a hypocrite
Why do we let this happen
Ignore the problems
Ignore we all have the same origins
Push people away
Don't let people stay
Afraid of a different belief or race
Fighting for the tiniest trace
Trace in history
History of what
Most psychopathic moment
Who wins the prize
Not the one saving the lives
No
The one getting revenge and causing more people to die
Living in a constant lie
Hatred is great
Your brain has been washed to say
I don't like anybody
If you can't relate
And don't understand how to listen and debate

That's correct
Spread hate
This world needs more of it
We need more blood
Blood's prettier than love

But who are they doing it for
Nobody knows and that's for sure
To a lot
You think you're the hero
Saving the day like when you're tired and get a coffee
from cafe nero
The thing is
Surely it's simple
Surely it's clear we all fucking live here
Maybe that woman believes in a different god
But how in any way does that make her odd
Be kind
Why can't we just all combine
Show your warmth
And you'll be greeted kindly
Back
Give that old man a smile
Maybe even talk to him for a while
Listen and express
And never any less
Then maybe we will all begin to understand nobody can
win
Against another man

We all have the same things keeping us alive
So instead let's hold hands and strive

Agnes Homer, 18

I Don't Know Where I've Got This Balance Wrong

– either a surfeit or a deficit of faith. Either way,
all my incredulous anger somehow elects
to curl itself around, back inwards,
sets to something far more solid: I refuse
(with a stubbornness I've been told is unbecoming,
unfeminine, inappropriate), right from the root,
to let this experience diminish me,
to beat my heart down

back into the easy shallow peace of cynicism,
keeping pace with the mute, drowsy rhythm
of our shitty broken culture
of forgetfulness, resignation.
I know this poem is like something a teenager
might write, too raging and too earnest,
but so what? Why is it so embarrassing
to allow ourselves to feel anything?
I don't want to be inured, resigned, despondent
in the face of all the senseless destruction and injustice,
the dull complicity. If I'm angry

then I have every fucking reason to be.
And that anger is beautiful: a great bright
thrust of energy, action, hope, confidence,
knowledge,
love.

Cate Chapman

A Love Letter

Dear Earth,

It is hard to write to you. Each time I turn to meet your gaze my heart rate quickens and my throat constricts. It's fear, it's remorse and it's grief, culminating deep in my chest.

Yet somehow it doesn't feel like the right time for an apology. I'm working hard for a world in which I hope I can say that to you properly. That means forging space to let remorse rise up and out. Welcoming the grief – and here beginning the search for remedy. If grief truly is the price we pay for love, then let this be a love letter.

To me you were, at first, red bottle-brush teasing the corner of my childhood window, the waking morn held in kookaburra laughter and lyrebird song, the stinging of that first bee thumbed in curiosity; tiny, spiky blades of grass on which I learned to walk and the grounds of a garden I later learned to nurture. And that just a fraction from the small corner where I originated. This all a love for an earth that offers herself up to my imagination and to my nourishment, body and soul.

What blossomed was an awareness of not just diversity of landscapes, but of life itself.

Diversity so rich it's staggering – and equally mournful to think that the world my parents were born into was doubly so.

If we are to curve this path, we must remember our place in this all.

Not other, but akin. Unified. A part of you, too.
I work each day so that remembrance comes soon.

All my love,
Ella

Oh, Arrogant and Impudent Beloved Child

who seeks to tame the world (as if you could!)
who runs afraid of all things wild –
fall headlong now into the chaos which you fear
and find me here

Oh, darling, tired and weary, screen-dead one
straddling platforms, ever searching to be whole
to have the revolution won
step into the dark of now's abyss:
stop, listen, feel my kiss

It's time, my love, to give up all this need to know
admit you can't and were not born to run the show
and, like the prodigal, with doubts and terrifying qualms
return to me, your mother, Earth:
I am here, with open arms

we are so close, we are each other's breathing out and in
I hold you, and the quiet beneath the din renews us
you find you're the love of love reflected in my ever-changing
    face:
to rise above the chaos you must first surrender to its grace

your tenderness cannot *but* respond
and hear the call beyond all guilt and grief
tending your own heart-scape brings the sweet relief
which touches, heals and acts with one immaculate
    intention:
to nurture our inseparable and felt connection.

Ever Yours,
The Earth
Liz Darcy Jones

The Act of Naming

Dear Earth,

We were outside in the dark when my daughter asked me how old you were.

'About 4.5 billion years old.'

'Oh. And what tree is that?'

Searching for the name of the tree silhouetted against the night sky I was, momentarily, disorientated, disconnected.

Earth. In English, your name begins in the throat and ends with tongue on teeth and lips. Earth, earth, earth, earth.

It travels through the mouth like breath. Say it over and over, it becomes like the sound you make from the effort of digging.

Where the name earth came from, its origin, we don't know. It meant ground? Soil? I have you under my nails as I return to work in the city, on the train. I was digging, planting potatoes, in our garden. Earth. To show my children where they come from. And where I will end up.

I want them to be able to see all that is around them, to know, to name what grows. Here. On you, earth. To name is to know. Because with naming comes a narrative. The word narrative comes from the word 'gnarus' which means 'knowing'. When we no longer have names we no longer have a story, we no longer 'know'; a connection is broken, the chain of events is ruptured and we become, perhaps, lost. Because telling stories is how we orientate ourselves in the world.

(And I know it takes 12.2 hectares of land to support each American citizen and 6.29 for each Briton. The figure for Burundi is just half a hectare. This is a story we have to tell.)

We would sleep on the ground, outside, on the hottest summer nights. When I was six. In sleeping bags, no tent, under the open sky. All of us in a row. My mother, father, brother and sister. Backs on the earth. I could feel the shape on my spine through the groundsheet. We would gaze at the stars, the immensity beyond our earth disconcerting.

'They're the ones that twinkle.'

'I know,' I lied. 'But what are their names?'

My brother knew much more than I did. Still does.

'Dunno. Too many ...'

'We know the names of the planets, don't we?'

'Yes. And the planets don't –'

'Twinkle, I know.'

'NO ... stay still.'

'Oh.'

The word planet comes from the Greek *planetai* 'wandering (stars)', and from *planathai* 'to wander'. Wandering stars. We were wanderers first. All over our own 'wandering star'. Every corner of it. In the dark we looked up and began to read the night sky. As John Berger says: 'Those who first invented and then named the constellations were storytellers. Tracing an imaginary line between a cluster of stars gave them an image and an identity. The stars threaded on that line were like events threaded on a narrative. Imagining the constellations did not of course change the stars, nor did it change the black emptiness that surrounds them. What it changed was the way people read the night sky.'

'There's Venus. And that cluster of stars are called the Pleiades.'

The earth, hard under the groundsheet, suddenly felt reassuring, supportive, certain.

But for a moment beside my daughter in the dark more than half a century later, I feel lost. The loss of knowing where you are when you have no name for what you see.

In his book *Landmarks*, Robert Macfarlane tells of this power of naming and equally the dispossession of losing names.

Such as the latest edition of the *Oxford Junior Dictionary*'s 'culling of words concerning nature ... no longer felt to be relevant to a modern-day childhood such as acorn, adder, ash, buttercup, cowslip, dandelion, fern, hazel, lark, newt, otter, pasture and willow. The words introduced included blockgraph, blog, broadband, celebrity, chatroom, MP3 player and voice-mail ... because this reflected the experience of modern-day childhood, in which seasons are no longer seen and the environment of rural, or wild nature, is disposable'.

To be unable to name is to be cut off because we cannot read. If we cannot read, we cannot connect or orientate ourselves or know that story you, our earth, is telling. Because you are insistently telling us an urgent narrative. Of loss. To notice this loss we must name it. The names must come back. To remind us. That we are all part of nature. Even as we gaze at our screens, apparently separate from the seasons, cowslips, newts, ferns and adders. We are all part of nature. All the time. And we cannot escape it, just as we cannot escape the planet.

'It's an ash.'

I can't believe I even hesitated on the name.

My daughter slips her hand into mine.

'And there above the branches, that little cluster of stars are called the Pleiades.'

She squeezes mine. And my heart skips a beat.

Skips a beat because we have declared a climate emergency. But this is not a word of panic. Emergency is a word whose root is *emergere*, 'arise, bring to light'. We are simply naming what we know 'to bring to light' the true narrative of what is happening to us now.

Earth. As I feel you under our feet and we look up at the night sky, I know that declaring an emergency is only the beginning. Now we need to act. Rediscover the names and craft them into chants of power that can change the world.

Simon McBurney

Everything

To the people who think that there's no point in trying, to the people who think that because we have done this we deserve to suffer the consequences. There's no point in giving up! In the past we have decided to turn away from mother nature's screams but not today! We will not let the earth we live on be destroyed so easily, we will try hard to save it from the very threat we created and see the world for its glory and its beauty.

Don't be the person who is standing back watching other people as they do the work.

Join the fight to save our world. If you don't then everything that we love about the world will slowly disappear.

Ollie Barnes, 12

Everything Is Connected

When I was young I would lie, pressed to the earth, eyes wide to the skies. I would watch you in your hundreds, criss-cross, hunt on the wing, layers of birds, some so high, seen only as dark commas against the blue, some so low to skim the reaching seeds of long grass.

When I was young I believed you carried the promise of summer sun on your wings.

When I was young I watched as you gathered mud in your mouth to build a home beneath the eaves of the houses of humans. Architect, potter, parent. I watched your shadow rise and fall, heard your children call, saw you answer them with food, watched them fledge.

When I was young I marvelled as you gathered, toward summer's end, small dots on wires like wild music, fast, furious rhythm, written against the sky.

When I was young I didn't know the distance you travelled, away from my winter, to warmer lands. I didn't know how you carried in your bodies the maps of the earth, the paths of the flight, scenting the land, knowing its shape, each rock and stream and tree and river and ocean. I didn't know how this knowledge was born in the egg, before egg became bird became flight, but I knew you were a miracle. Every single soul.

Once some believed you slept all winter beneath the ice in ponds.

Once some believed the earth is flat.

Now some believe climate change is fiction.

But now, when I lie on my back in the long grass, breathing its scent, eyes wide to the sky, my heart still lifts to see your wings, though you are now so few. Each year more sky, more space, and each single swallow more precious for that.

And I still marvel to see you gather as autumn scents the air, still writing your wild music on the wires in the sky. But now the music is a lament, more space between each note, a song of praise and loss, an elegy for the ghosts of gone birds.

And I know, I cannot live without you.

Jackie Morris

Loss

False Alarm

Sometimes I have this dream.

I'm going for a hike and discover a remote farmhouse on fire.

Children are calling for help from the upper windows. So I call the fire brigade. But they don't come, because some mad person keeps telling them that it is a false alarm.

The situation is getting more and more desperate, but I can't convince the firemen to get going.

I cannot wake up from this nightmare.

Stefan Rahmstorf
Head of Earth System Analysis
Potsdam Institute for Climate Impact Research

What have we done to the Planet?

I don't know about you,
but this is how I feel
about Mother nature.
We have become Mother
Natures enemy.
The Planet is dying.
Mother Nature is Crying
Out for help.
we need to Start Working
together.
you may think the planet
is not crying but it is.
Mother Nature is inside of us,
She is all around us. She
made us be alive.
For if She were not alive,
we would not live.
We must thank her
every day.

Tabitha. Ravula
Age 7½

Finding Dory

To my favourite, funny little people,

What can I say, now that it's too late?

I can tell you the obvious: that I'm sorry, that I tried.

I can tell you how sorry I am, that it ate me up. That even as we sat in bed with the nightlight on, reading together about coral reefs and finding Dory, I knew there was not much time left for those bright and beautiful places.

I can tell you that I tried, that even though it felt hopeless, I wasn't going to quit. I can tell you that this is why we always took the train, why I pestered politicians, why we changed what we ate, why I got myself arrested that time.

But what I really want you to know: that the hardest thing was living through a time when we could have turned this around, but that most people just carried on as if it didn't matter.

There will be a thousand explanations for this. You'll hear that people were selfish, that we were trapped in a consumer culture, that our politicians were craven servants of fossil fuels, that the media didn't keep us informed, too preoccupied with dance contests, fashions and trivia.

There is something in all of this, but I want you to know what it felt like at the time. It felt like a dream, where everything seemed so normal, but where under the surface there was a horrible and brutal truth we all pretended didn't exist. Hardly anyone even spoke about climate change and the destruction of the natural world. If you did, more often than not the conversation would be shut down, familiar devices pulled out of nowhere to dismiss, sidetrack and silence your concerns.

And outside, the world – the thoughtless, concrete and metal, fume-choked, all-consuming human world – rumbled on, deaf to the warnings and unwilling to lift a finger.

I want to tell you that I am sorry, and that I tried.

Your dad,
Stuart

Cruise control

The weather will change,
We'll think it malicious.
Speak hurricanes' names and worry in secret.
The waves will build somewhere way out in the ocean,
And flatten whole towns when they break on the beaches.

It won't be enough. We'll plough on
The mightiest we've ever been.
Standing like gods on the shoulders of history.
Or tossing our curls in the sun.

We'll stare down at the screens in our hands
And smile at the photos. *Didn't we laugh.*
Strange voices will sing from street corners.
Powerful men will mumble it into the backs
Of the people they fuck. *This is the end.*

Health and safety slogans will resonate like ancient proverbs.
Don't use the lifts in the case of fire.
Make yourself aware of your nearest exit.
We'll bury our heads in the sand of our lovers.

The waters will boil in the oceans.
Dead things will float on the waves.
The ice caps will thicken to slush puppies
As hurricanes twist
Like boxers in sleeping bags, trying to throw punches.

There'll be fires in the forests, floods in the cities.
And men too rich to swim will die.
The skin on our children will toughen and harden.
And still we will debase ourselves
For that piece of land or mineral
That rock or bomb or golden egg
That might allow one dying person to imagine
They are worth more than another.

Kae Tempest

We Humans

The first thing we need to grasp is that this situation is bigger than what we understand, it is on a larger scale than anything we have ever faced before. It makes our human wars, our economy and social issues seem like such small irrelevant problems which, in the face of what is heading our way, they are.

Let me ask you this: what use will your smart car be when there is no longer any clean air to breathe because we have cut all the trees down? What use will a 'successful' job be when there are simply no more resources? We are all still so stuck in all of our human problems and issues; fighting wars against each other; trying to keep our economy afloat; but what use will any of that be when food and water begin to run out or when there are sudden devastating weather outbursts and consistently rising sea levels and the remains of what used to be ice caps, when all the soil is too toxic to grow on any more from all the pesticides that have been sprayed on it for so many years, when all the rivers and water sources are also contaminated with toxic chemicals. This is heading our way.

This is imminent and absolutely real.

Something that the majority of people still fail to understand is the fact that everything is connected. Everything. Our planet is like one big organism, it's one huge ecosystem and an ecosystem, like the mechanics of a watch, has exactly all the right pieces for it to keep running smoothly. Change one tiny cog, put one tiny part out of place and the whole system collapses.

Everything is part of everything and we humans are not somehow separate. We rely on nature, on our environment just as much as everything else, and what got us into this mess in the first place was the lack of understanding of this; us thinking that we as humans are somehow superior and deserve to take whatever we wish and as much as we wish from our environment without giving anything back. We humans thinking we are superior is the root of the problem.

Things we would never consider doing to ourselves, things that we view as horrific and barbaric, toxic or destructive, we happily do to everything else without a second thought.

Nicola Espitalier Noel, 16

The Act of Incremental Vanishing

Our Earth,

When I stop and listen I can hear your ice caps melting. Not the expected plink, plonk but a steady tremolo. It's a bit like free-running dominoes, like paddling bathwater with one's toes, like an elongated sigh. There used to be a hotline for it. Honestly, we could once listen live to the Icelandic glacier in the act of incremental vanishing. Now, it's an archive version. This plays in the gallery. Symphonic. The world's longest swansong. It moves me. In the other room Beethoven plays too; beamed back from your moon the broken 'Moonlight' Sonata floods through, flawed and pockmarked, and in the gaps your tearful tune joins in a duet of the dead and dying. I close my eyes and imagine I am swimming in a cave while the water is steadily rising. Outside, in the white, I picture ice budding into beads, pooling, forming tunnels from hairline cracks, chasing itself in rivulets, diving deep into the sea. Irrevocably gone. I walk along the shore, following the tide line. And when I get home I know this sound still pounds like blood spilling from a severed vein. Sometimes it's hard to say or pointless to list all the bits that are wrong about people and the problems we precipitate so I'm sticking with this one, prescient song. We don't have long but what I want to say is that I hear you.

Yours,
Jessica Taggart Rose

Dear Animals

Dear Animals,
The world use to be a safe place for you.
I am sorry we have ruined that.

Elliotte Mitchell, 12

Nichollsia borealis

Like you I am a predator. Unlike you, I am no longer here. Most of you do not know how we were once pushed by the razor-sharp winds that blew across the Old Red Continent. The waters emptied as they flowed from the newly formed salty seas. They crossed slabs of inland shale and crashed into caves of anhydrite crystals. Some of us lived in the dark back then, others kept their eyes wide open seeing the sky's bright light leaking through our ceiling of brine. You were not around to see us. We were marvels. Treasures. Gifts from deep inside the earth formed in the shape of things you would come to call reptiles and in your myths we became monsters. We grew slowly, making our way down the clear rivers freshly forged through forests of ferns, islands of moss and clumps of seed-rich soils. Like so many of our brothers and sisters, we died out when the mountains rose, crashing and tilting the earth and crushing us under their weight. We left our flesh, our eyes, our skin and our skeletons embedded in rock and in the hardening sap of pine trees. This was the way of things. Our rich remains blended with the spruce and willow bark, the muskeg and the soil. Slowly, over millions of years, we became the bracken soup, the bitumen, the tar, the oil.

The water that used to flush out our ancestors from deep inside the earth runs into the poison tailings of water that is no longer the water that gave us life. Our bodies had been preserved in the once frozen ground which is melting to reveal our bones, our teeth, our sharp claws used to pry open the shells of the giant molluscs that floated below us in the ancient salty seas. Our children spoke to the people who lived here in Athabasca, but now our descendants can no longer breathe long enough to speak. They are not marvels; they are mutants. Eventually you will join us in this heavy, heavy water that is not water. You will not thank us. You will ask, 'Why?' and we will not have the breath to answer you. You have taken it from us. We – you and I – will be as mute as the rocks made from bones and stardust.

Joanna Pocock

A Place I Call Home

Dear Earth,

I write on behalf of my family, on behalf of my country and the 31 million residents currently living in a place I call home, Peru.

A place where my family had to be woken up in the middle of the night to evacuate their home because of the earthquakes that are affecting their day-to-day lives.

A place where the people with the least money are the ones that suffer the most.

And yet, a big part of *our* society continues to turn a blind eye, as climate change isn't 'affecting us' – or even completely denies the fact that climate change is a thing.

The sad truth is that most of the time the people and businesses who contribute to global warming the most aren't the ones who are suffering right now – and as they aren't the ones suffering right now climate change must not exist, *right*?

Tell me how can we turn a blind eye to climate change when it is responsible for 150,000 deaths each year around the world?

As if my natives and indigenous people from the Amazon are just obstacles or burdens, not people, like you and me.

Whose homes are being taken away from them by major corporations that believe deforestation is just about cutting trees and do not dare to think about the consequences that it has on the hundreds of species of plants, insects, birds and mammals that vanish each day, for ever.

Because, somehow, making money from businesses and properties has become more valuable than life itself.

Therefore, I apologise to you, earth, and to the millions of people suffering currently because of the 'controversial' topic we call climate change.

Daniela Torres Perez, 17

Small Islands Everywhere

Dear Small Islands Everywhere,

I think of you often. Many of you swim in oceans of water and have been happy to do so for aeons. Until now. Now the seas of time lap at your shores. And time is ebbing away as you float suspended. Without life buoys or influence over waves that augur drowning. The melting ice. The rising waters.

Where is the lifeboat? How many will it hold? Will it be overwhelmed by the swell as you abandon the ship of your lives in search of safe harbour? Will the drawbridge of safety be drawn up as you float ideas of salvage or rescue? Will hands that are drowning not waving be hoisted from the flood?

I was born on the small islands of St Kitts-Nevis. Now I inhabit a big one – Great Britain. Where the power of the Industrial Revolution gave birth to material consumption. Like a pendulum global consumption has swung to its zenith. It is way past time for the tide of consumer souls to drain and flow to a spirit level that slakes our thirst without submerging us. Or the earth will witness such movement of islands small to big as no Ark could accommodate.

The waters of time are storming. To keep Small Islands safe let the big ones learn to live smaller.

Yours sincerely,
Tyrone Huggins

Why Should We Care?

My dad said that we
should worry about our own life, not the rest of
the world.

It won't affect us.

But I disagree with that
because in the year 2050 the world will be
completely different, in a bad way.

Between
10,000 and 100,000 species are becoming extinct
each year so I *will* worry about the world now.

Haydon Bushell, 12

Letter to a Starling

We forget that you were once as common as coal; little coal-
   black bird.
Stumpy, dumpy. The wire-dotter; pylon-swarmer.
Camped out on our ledges and trees, screaming England's
   towns down.
Noisy as a classroom on the last day of term.
We forget that you once shimmered through frozen air;
   ripple bird.
Shape-shifter, dusk-dancer. Murmurer; sky-writer,
Endlessly becoming in the darkening gold: animals, patterns,
   waves.
And how we, wonder-struck, witnessed your nightly unity
   against death.
We forget that you stayed true; loyal little bird.
Roof-flocker; aerial-clinger, when the rest up and left.
And how, up close, you carried the constellations in your
   feathers,
Iridescent purples, greens and blues, the rare hues of petrol
   on water.
We forget that you were once as common as coal; little coal-
   black bird.
And that your blackening of our streets and whistling
   through our chimneystacks,
Your smoke-like swirling in the skies, was an olive branch
   from heaven.

Yet in the mad pursuit of a spotless life, we believed you
    plague.
We forget that in loss it's the little things that leave the
    largest holes;
And that, all along, you were drawing patterns for us to live
    by:
Community bird, collaborator, congregator, conversation
    bird.
You, accepter bird, come-together bird.
Crowd bird. YOLO bird.
The dance-like-no-one's-watching bird,
Over town and field, city and sea.
Beauty-beyond-compare bird. Modest bird,
Youth bird. Joy bird.
We forget that you were once as common as coal,
And how that makes your scarcity more keenly felt.
And how losing you is devastating,
A hole in our sky and soul.
For it signifies a greater loss in us.

Rob Cowen

A Frog Shrivelled in the Dust

To the gods of the world, from one of the unnamed, a letter:

Honoured Sirs,
Something has happened. Hard to say what. My mind, my small mind, registers certain events. A hard thing came down on a beetle. A frog shrivelled in the dust. The air became more difficult to breathe, my body felt heavier, my wings stiffened: who knows? Did this happen overnight, or has it been going that way for years? All I can say for sure is that life is much harder than it was. The sun looks angry, the old trees have ceased to talk. Flying about my daily business I notice a shortage of the brilliant foods on which I used to feast; at the same time there are heavy rains and many wildfires. I have a sense of calamity. I am light and humble. I do not feel strong any longer. Yesterday I crawled into a hole in the ground and I am not sure whether it is safe to come out. There was once music in the undergrowth, but now only the occasional creaking noises. Where is everyone? I think things may be coming to an end. Please tell me, is it a delusion? If it is not a delusion, please tell me the truth. Without the truth there is no hope for anyone. I am frightened here. Do you exist any longer? Is anyone listening?

Christopher Nicholson

A Letter to the Dying

Dear Earth,

We have never been formally introduced, but I like to think we know each other well. I talk to you all the time in my head, so this letter shouldn't be hard to write, right? But I guess it's always hard to know what to say to the dying.

I work with young people, getting them out of the classroom and into nature, and showing them what's out there – showing them what you've got to offer. I take them to the river and show them the delicate mayfly nymphs with their feathery gills waving, to the coast to see the tough grasses getting their roots into the sand dunes, to the woods to try to name some of the many growing things. I do this because I love it, and because it took me so long to find you on my own. So much time spent feeling displaced and directionless, not realising that what I was missing was you. I'd like to help someone skip a few of those years.

But sometimes I wonder if I'm doing the right thing; if all I'm really doing is helping those kids to see your infinite complexity and beauty, just in time to understand what they've lost. I probably won't have children of my own. There are some things a child shouldn't have to see: the collapse of civilisation in the midst of ecological ruin is one of them. I can't offer a child a future. That's something that's been taken from me – from us.

I'm afraid for those young people, as I am for myself. I don't know how long I can go on living this comfortable life, with my nice job in my city by the sea.

When I was younger, if teen life ever got me down, I used to cheer myself up by walking along the river. I used to tell myself I could cope with anything as long as I had the wind in the trees, a sky full of birdsong, the golden grass in the meadow, humming with life. I made these things my bedrock. They gave me the stability to deal with the world. I believed they could never be taken away. To live through what's ahead of us without even these to rely on is a fate I don't know how to face.

I don't know what will happen now, to me or to you. I don't believe in heaven. I hope when the time comes I'll go to the same place as the small tortoiseshell butterfly, the Scottish wildcat, the wind in the trees by the river, and the creatures that buzz in the meadow.

But I want to offer the young a better hope than that.

With love,
Isobel Bruning

I Didn't Even Know!

Dear Earth,

Recently, I have realised that we as humans are destroying you.

You used to be all beautiful, clear skies and growing trees. A happy place to be. But we have made your skies dirty and smoky and chopped down the trees. Not such a happy place to be after all.

I am not going to sit here, typing on the computer, and say that I knew what was going on. Because that would be a lie. Honestly, I had no clue that sea animals, birds and our ocean were dying because of us! We are the reason that turtles are choking on bottle caps, birds are picking up plastic folders thinking they are fish and feeding it to their babies. I had no clue the ocean, where we could swim happily and animals used to have a decent home, is now a place where the plastic now lays.

People may not know they are killing these animals. Hey – I didn't even know! But that shouldn't be the case. When we are watching the news, we see things about *everything* but the detrimental effect we have on the environment. A few days ago we could probably recite every little thing about Brexit, and maybe one thing about these dreadful matters. This shouldn't be the case! There are worse things happening in this world than someone robbing the mini market, or someone's dog ran away or some celebrity couples breaking up.

In fifty years' time, these animals that we know and love may not be here. My grandchildren may never see elephants or tigers or sloths. They will never know what a rainforest is, or clear skies, or beautiful lakes. But we can change that.

They deserve to have the same experience that I have at the moment. But if we keep doing what we are doing, everything will vanish in front of us. First the land, then the animals, then us. We don't know it, but by destroying our world, we are slowly destroying humankind.

We are not terrible people. We are only human after all. But we can make a change.

I may be only twelve years old, but I care, and you should too.

Saibh Da Silva, 12

Amnesia

I did not mean to kill the last of the eagles.
I just forgot to feel my wings soaring high above the cliffs and
    crags.

I did not mean to kill the last of the salmon.
I just forgot the thrill of leaping through the surging foam.

I did not mean to kill the last of the buffalo.
I just forgot to feel the fear of galloping with the herd.

I did not mean to kill the last of the spiders.
I just forgot to feel the geometry and sway of weaving a silken
    web.

I did not mean to kill the last of the foxgloves.
I just forgot how it feels to glisten with mirror orbs of
    morning dew.

I did not mean to kill the last of the honey bees.
I just forgot the sound of the thrum at the heart of the hive.

I did not mean to kill the last of the oak trees.
I just forgot how it feels to stand for a hundred years.

I did not mean to wreck our home.
I just forgot how to dwell with you.

Even when you told me what would happen, I forgot.
Even when you tell me what is happening, I forget.
Even when you show me what has happened, I forget.

Please remind me.
Please remind me.

Justin Roughley

The Night Toby Denied Climate Change

We were sitting like a group of Vervet monkeys*
beside a fire in a bucket, casting shadows, trying to keep
    warm.
Above us the stars trailed with
Light from where they were no longer.
And I remembered all the other times, when
we had said: How can we stop
The sudden heat? The melting and the floods?
The yearly losses of birds, the lack of cuckoo song,
The hunger of displacement.
In my head I made a list of everything we'd lose,
Cornflower, dock, radish, oak summer,
Earwigs, bees, crows, potatoes, cabbages.
But it was far too long. Then I remembered that
being animal, I could live on berries,
green leaves, roots from underground
grown in a patch of earth.

Then Graham said, For goodness sake! Look at this ring of
    firelight.
We need to make more fires and circles for the soul
Across the beaches and the hills
Lanterns for Gaia,
Not just a label, or a clever name
But light and conversations, to bring changes.
See all those others, across the distance.

And Toby shrugged and grinned and said,
'OK. I'll carry on!'
(Luckily it was December, the cold frost time called winter,
That has snow,
and it still mattered to hope.)

Clare Crossman

*Vervet monkeys are an endangered species.

The First Earth Day

I was there, you know, at your age,
For the first Earth Day.
I stood up to my parents.
Told them we needed to get rid of our cars.
Stood there against the uproarious laughter
And declared I would never have a car!
I meant it, too.
I knew better than them.
I thought I could do it –
Just walk away from it all –
Be mighty! Be the Change!
Simple.
I didn't see it coming –
The powerful forces
That would eat away at my determination,
Wear down my resolve,
One little missed bus at a time,
One non-existent bus at a time,
One freezing wait at a bus stop at a time;
The relentless slog against the elements
And a system designed to wear you down.
To corrode your will,
Waiting until it's frayed around the edges
To surround you with the song of the sirens.
Those silky voices that sing
Sweet nothings in your ear,

Promising endless ease and plush,
So nice, so fluffy, so THERE.
'Why resist? Come on, give in!
You know you want to.
Why carry on with this crazy ideal of yours?
Look, there's plenty here for you.'

Giving in is a gradual thing,
Almost imperceptible.
One little change here,
One little excuse there,
Made while navigating the rocky road
Of terrible choices.

And now,
Fifty years later,
I drive faster than the speed limit,
Unable to stay awake in the garden with Jesus,
Like the silly disciples nodding off
Before the crucifixion.

Mary Benefiel

A Letter to the Earth (If It Can Read?)

I am in a city. I am sitting outside but I've brought the inside with me so that I can write to you. I'm not sure you can read. I'm not sure that writing matters but it's something I can do so I do it. It is the first outside day of the year but I am inside the city and so the inside is everywhere, cordoning off space, making it into shapes that once weren't there but that we, or I maybe, are unable to remember. The café and the bus place me in a rectangle between themselves and, now out of sight, I simply forget the green beyond.

I like how I look today. I feel allowed. I run my mind down my body and defend everything I'm wearing: jumper: charity shop; T-shirt: M&S 100 per cent ethical cotton. I blink at the thought that the label might not tell the truth or the truth might not mean what I need it to mean to defend myself. But it's a small wobble before I put my faith firmly back in M&S where it belongs. Jeans: high street. High street chain yes, but I am making the most of them. Making the most of what they cost. I make a note to buy better jeans next time. There will be a next time won't there? Socks: threadbare, origins forgotten; pants: microfibre ... What is that? Where will that go to die? Perhaps my pants will outlive me? Still, it's nice to think of some kind of legacy.

I think about a book I read recently where a girl climbs through a dumpster doing the food shop for the week. I had felt a bit sick. The pretty girl's pretty mouth dripping at the corner with the juice of a once-was tomato. I remember my neat plastic-wrapped tomatoes, red and ripe, losing their flavour in the fridge. Perhaps my rectangle is a dumpster? But, roomier than hers, with its sides stretched so far apart I'm able to forget the space between them is a trash can. There's a veg box being delivered today. Not a box, a bag. The vegetables come from the farm in a recyclable brown paper bag. That's what the website says. So there's no need to be angry. What could be more calming than a brown paper bag? I think when I get home I'll sit down and breathe in and out into it slowly until I forget about tomatoes and where microfibre goes to die.

I'll watch a documentary. That's what I'll do. I'll go back inside and watch a documentary about cow shit; or palm oil; or turtles breathing through straws; or the temperature rising. I'll make a list of promises to do better and then when I've inked all the paper in the house I'll go to a bar and talk out new excuses to break those promises, those little life changes, and the people I gather round me will shrug and nod and agree with me because we live in a city made up of little rectangles, because we can't remember the space that used to be, because our pants will outlive us, because we say your name in such a way you've become just an idea really. And really, *really* it's somebody else's fault, somebody more powerful's problem, somebody else has to fix it. I'm just rummaging around in the dumpster and you, you can't even read.

Jessica Siân

Sorry

What is it they say – 'Sorry is the hardest word'?

Well, I'm sorry.

I am.

I'm sorry for what we've done to you.

I am sorry that we didn't listen to the warnings.

I'm sorry that I put my trust in the media that is more obsessed with fashion and football, and reality TV, with where the Dow Jones is, with game shows, with baking, with putting a positive spin on 71 degree heat in February with a 'Wow, what a great opportunity for ice cream sellers.' I'm sorry for all of it.

I'm sorry that when I first heard about what was happening, I looked away. No, I listened away if you want to be factually correct. I remember it still. It was the radio. I heard someone say on the radio news, on a Monday morning, that 'Scientists are concerned that the world is heating up due to a build-up of so-called greenhouse gases emitted by the burning of fossil fuels that may warm the earth to potentially dangerous levels,' and I thought, That's scary! And then they added, 'But there is disagreement from other scientists who say, "There's no need to worry, it won't happen for hundreds of years and will most likely benefit the planet and make the UK as warm as the Costa Del Sol."'

And I breathed out. I'm sorry I was so uneducated about this world to know that where there is money there is spin, there are lies, there is false balance and I didn't investigate and

102

find out that those scientists were being paid by oil companies to confuse us all, something they did well.

I'm sorry that I just ticked it off my list of things I needed to be concerned about, like which clothes to wear this summer and where to go on holiday and I went and read a magazine instead. Maybe it was ten tips on how to be happy. I was always looking for tips on how to be happy. I'm looking for them again now.

I'm sorry that I had a friend who said I'm really worried about this and you need to understand this better and you need this book, and I didn't, and I just thought, No, I want a thriller about a girl who disappears. I don't want to read that, and I relied on newspapers and journalists. I mean, can you imagine, something so stupid as relying on newspapers and journalists. And I should know, I am one. I'm sorry I didn't pick up a book.

I'm sorry that when I was at dinner parties, so many dinner parties, so many events, so many cocktail parties where the subject would come up and people said to me, 'It's not true, I don't believe it,' or 'It's green crap,' or 'It's about taxes,' or 'It's been created to scare us,' and I didn't challenge them.

I didn't educate myself enough to say, 'But NASA say it *is* happening, it *is* man-made and so do an overwhelming majority of the world's leading scientists.' And when they said, 'Yes, but it's a natural cycle,' I wasn't educated enough to say, 'For fuck's sake, who do you think taught you that the climate changes naturally?'

I'm sorry I didn't challenge your father when he would shut down conversations by saying, 'Ah well, India and China are building dozens of coal power stations, there's no point us doing anything.' I'm sorry I didn't say, 'OK, we'll just accept the kids are going to burn then.'

I'm sorry that instead I just said, 'Yeah,' and I watched the TV again.

I'm sorry I never said, 'That's my children's future you are talking about.'

These are my children.

You are my children.

I'm so sorry.

Matthew Todd

On an Ancient Carving

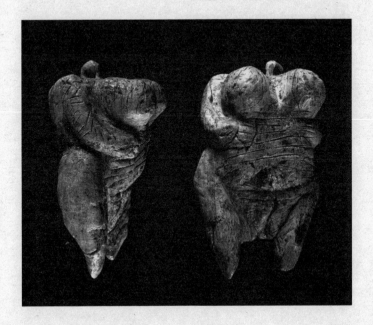

Ivory broken from a mammoth tooth
and shaped some forty thousand years ago
into the goddess-body of the earth.

Revealed: the wide, child-bearing hips,
the narrow portal through which life
arrives, the bounty of her breasts,

and all the lines that time has etched
across her skin, like surface scratches
on a glacier-driven lump of stone.

And we, the wastrels of a golden age,
do well to stand in awe before
this wise, indomitable ancestor –

our Mother Earth who gives us everything
and is the goddess who will *for*give nothing.

Lindsay Clarke

Patient E

Dear Dr Now,

I'm writing to you with great concern regarding our common patient, E.

Since her hospitalisation, her condition has weakened continuously despite all our efforts. Our treatment still focuses on sedative medication and painkillers, combined with therapy sessions three times per week. Twice, during the last year, her insurance approved an extended stay in the rehabilitation centre for abuse victims, but it seems that they have not contributed to her recovery. The patient is complying with all our advice with patience, but our methods are not successful. I find myself wondering if our initial diagnosis, F.2015 – Change, was given too optimistically, or completely false altogether. Without wanting to point fingers, I am looking at all the information we were given by the lab and I'm not convinced they're correct.

What worries me deeply is that she shows signs of a grave personality disorder, which I cannot explain. Her cognitive functions, for example her understanding of periods of time, like the change of seasons, or her memory of certain words (especially adverbs like 'by °s', 'carefully', 'little by little') seem to deteriorate. Furthermore, she, who we got to know as a calm and friendly character, now shows raging emotional outbursts. For example, during the last month she repeatedly flooded the toilet that she hides in when she starts crying. When our nurses finally succeeded in opening the door, she kept sobbing inconsolably for hours, until the antidepressants eventually got the situation under control. On the contrary side, she started to express her anger by burning plants in our hospital garden and running around manically to produce storms, as she has declared to her therapist. Our efforts to alleviate her panic attacks, by providing her with constant light and communication possibilities, were in vain. During an episode of desperation, she has even killed her fish (we allowed her to keep a personal aquarium in the room, hoping the sight of her so beloved animals would support her therapy progress).

I must confess, I suspect strongly that our treatment of E is completely wrong. Not only are we unable to stop the decline of her energy and physiological balance, we also seem to fuel a fever that is increasing steadily. Having said all that, I am positive that her condition is not palliative just yet.

But I really need to know what to do. I'm willing to do the whole assessment procedure over again, reverse all our decisions and treat her accordingly. As I am obviously not able to do this on my own, I ask you for your cooperation, your expertise, your help.

I will not give up on our patient. I will not give up on her.

Sincerely,
Dr Human,
Head of Climate Emergency

Fracture

It is the year of fracture. Of starting to understand.

It is spring.

I write in a wooden cabin at the bottom of the garden with a view over the pond. The dragonflies come there. There is flag iris and gunnera. There are newts.

I have a daughter. She plays in the garden, she loves the sand-pit. She is two years old.

I am writing a book – researching for a story – and one bright morning I type in a phrase.

How long till societal collapse …

And then I read. About locked-in tipping points, the non-linear, graphs that are jagged, saw-toothed. Unpredictable. Terrifying.

I look out, at my daughter, to where she plays in the sand.

—

All spring, as the world greens and blooms, I try to talk about it, this new story, which has fractured my own – my sense of what a story should be. And people listen and nod and agree and glaze a little but mostly say yes, yes, I know it's terrible. But it might not happen. It might not.

The spring becomes summer and the summer is hot.

We drive to the coast and eat on the beach and swim and agree it is amazing, this weather – to be able to plan things! To be able to say, Let's meet on the beach next Friday too! Our children love the warmth. They run around with nothing on. We grow used to it. We look at each other and smile, and grow brown and happy in the sun.

But the sun does not cease. The garden grows brown too. The gunnera grows crispy and dies. The pond dries up. Where do the newts go? They have disappeared.

We agree it would be good to have a bit of rain. The rain does not come.

—

The year turns, becomes autumn. Each morning, it seems, there is more bad news: twelve years to change course, the insect apocalypse – they have gone, apparently, while no one was looking. Disappeared. No one knows where.

It is November and dark at four o'clock. The year is contracting. There is fear in the house. I read paper after paper. Papers that tell us we may only have ten years left. That we should start to prepare. To adapt. To imagine starving to death, really quite soon.

I have a friend who is staying with me, and she and I stand in the kitchen in the dim mornings and talk in hushed voices as though afraid of being overheard.

What would we do? If it came to it? She is a doctor and she mentions cyanide. When she talks of cyanide I keep seeing that bit in *Downfall* – that film of the last days of Hitler? – where they are all in the bunker and they know it is the end and Goebbels's wife is putting the cyanide pills in her children's mouths while they are sleeping and then cracking their jaws to release the poison. Crack crack crack. The look on her face. All of them in their little bunks.

I think, Are we really talking about this? Standing here, either side of the butcher's block, two middle-aged, middle-class women – talking about the possible end?

—

I look at places online. Wales. Connemara. Places with water, with rivers, a well.

I say to my husband, We have to buy land. Sell up. Go to Ireland. Buy some acres. Learn to farm. Bore holes. All of that.

My husband shakes his head, he does not seem afraid. He says, *We have always lived in uncertain times.*

—

I had therapy once, when I was trying to have a child. I tried to have a child for years and years. Sometimes I would feel aberrant, outside of nature. Sometimes I would wonder if this is how the earth felt, old and sad and sick with grief, struggling to bring forth life.

Anyway, this therapist, I said to her, I love my mother. She's amazing. She's an earth mother. She baked and she cooked and she made and she held us.

And she looked at me, this therapist, and nodded in that way they have.

Mothers have many sides, she said. They are not just benign.

Mothers can turn. Be jagged, saw-toothed, unpredictable. Furious. Uncontainable. Unreliable. Mothers can turn.

—

I have begun to pray. I find myself praying. By trees. On earth.

—

I lie in my bed with my daughter beside me. I like to sleep beside her, these nights. To feel her animal warmth. She should sleep in her own bed, but it is nice like this, burrowed down together, as though we are in a den. And she is a cub. Outside – beyond the windows, the owls call to each other, over the dark fields, hunting in the night.

Anna Hope

Dear Earth,

What to say?

On the one hand everything is dust and air and will continue. On the other hand we have our human awareness, our consciousness, our narratives and our struggles.

And then there is my womb and the little boy with his father's smile who lives in my mind and asks to be born.

It seems the only thing to do now is to fight for justice, regardless of outcome. In the face of extinction this seems potentially incredibly naive and yet – what else is there to do in this moment with the weight of all human history asking for a reason to have existed?

So, I have put myself on BirthStrike and instead of making a family, I fight lovingly but determinedly in the hope we can achieve harmony in life before the disintegration of death brings its own kind of restoration and balance.

While I live I will give myself this meaning by joining the movement for love and unity where I am most needed – on the street.

I can see walls and roofs covered in moss and flowers, I can see my boy playing, I see you in love with us and we with you and each other.

Courage and compassion until the last,

Blythe

For Aoife

February and it's too warm to wear a coat. We feed the groggy bees with sugar-water from a Calpol syringe.

You say, *I'm frightened; I'm frightened of this weather and I'm frightened of what the world will be like when I'm older.*

And I'm frightened too. My body's frightened of this little summer; it's out of time and out of tune. I'm frightened of what the world will be like for you.

I say hopeful things, that humanity can do better; that we will get our act in order. That we will have to.

We get our own small act in order. We take the train, go vegan, refuse plastic, buy less and less.

But that is tiny. We are tiny. We watch parliament cut itself to pieces. We watch the cars belt past our house, planes tear across the sky. We feed the bees. And we are afraid.

Jo Baker

Procrastination

19 March 2050

Dear Future Generations,
Sorry. We didn't get there in time. We were too late. Except we had time. We had *time* to change. Instead, we put it off, waiting for the miracle that never came to come and always reassuring ourselves with the phrase: we will do it tomorrow. Tomorrow never came. And I'm sorry to tell you that because of us and the destruction we caused, there won't be many tomorrows left.

Sorry.

Sorry that in this mess of a world we left you, time is dwindling. I would say enjoy the time that remains – except that vast views are now block buildings, open air is clogged with chemicals, rushing rivers are furious floods and trees ... Trees are gone.

Sorry that instead of seeing trees as graceful homes for now extinct species, we view them as nothing but paper; money. Great big money-making machines. A whole forest; trees originally laden with branches of bountiful blossoms become drenched in shimmering gold coins in our greedy, human eyes. So we chop them down, using ugly, looming machines to rip them apart at the rate of forty football pitches a minute, tearing down branches, digging desperately for any trace of riches whatsoever.

And what did we do with that money? I'll tell you. We built cars; polluting the air mile by mile. We built factories, towering over masked faces, coughing and spluttering – emitting vast clouds of thick, dark pollution-chemicals filling the once clear air, coming over us like a suffocating blanket, draping itself over any clear sky. It's warm. Too warm. Too hot – melting the ice caps.

Sorry. Sorry that the ice is no more. Sorry that the water is rising; lapping at our ankles now but it will surge. It will flood. It will take lives. Your lives. Sorry.

Sorry for draining the beauty of life from your eyes. Sorry for using the very earth as a personal credit card with no limit. Sorry that your view from your grey, block apartment consists of a polluted sky, concrete pavements and monstrous diggers, churning up any remaining blades of grass. Sorry that time slipped through our fingers.

Katie Skiffington, 13

Letter to an Endling

Dear Esa,

Your name Esa means 'the only one' in human language: 'the lonely one'.

After your last heartbeat, a world will be gone – for ever. Not, people think, an important one. Only yours, but your only world.

After your last flight, a freedom will be lost – for ever. Not, people think, an important one. Only yours, but your only freedom.

After your last song, a category of music will be silenced – for ever. Not, people think, an important one. Only yours, but your only song and the only one you ever wanted to hear sung back to you. For while you live, you can sing your female laughingthrush call all you like and no male will ever answer you and you will never know why.

Your story happened because of the slaughter of songbirds. In flocks once, then trapped, traded and caged, sentenced to solitary, forced to sing solo. Bird-sorrow for a status symbol.

You are a nervous bird. In the photograph I have of you, you look frightened. Your eyes are an orange circle with a black centre, and you don't like being in the eyeline of your keepers. You are easily stressed, and would rather be hidden in deep foliage, tucked in thickets of forests.

You have never wanted to call attention to yourself, except for a mate, but now you have the cachet of true tragedy. Your kind, the rufous-fronted laughingthrush, sub-species slamat-ensis, is named as the world's next most likely extinction. You, exactly you, Esa, one single individual bird, are the last. Your death will mark its extinction. You, Esa the lonely one, as the last individual of your kind, are an endling.

This is what extinction sounds like: the silencing of song that should have been for ever yours.

For ever yours.

Jay Griffiths

there's this moment
when you find out
you realise, that your mother could die
and you know, you know you'll do anything
anything
to make it right
she's sick
and her body, that gave life and joy and promise and futures
it has given too much
her body has no more to give
appointments, lifestyle changes, treatments and medications
operations
you do what it takes.
but soon,
there's a moment
the moment when you find out
you learn
you accept
you know
that none of it will work
the choices are gone
everything. slows.
and all you can do is sit
and love her
until she isn't here any more.

Ann Lowe

The Age of Catastrophes

Dear Earth,

Give us the suffering we deserve. The pandemic you sent us is a sad beginning. Too often we have been saved by the benevolence of the universe. When salvation comes easily, we do not learn.

We only learn through suffering. We have become too spoilt, too stupid, too self-regarding. We fancy ourselves as gods. But we are children of death and immortality. We are nothing but wonder woven into mortal flesh.

It is time for our flesh and our dreams to be tried. It is time for us to undergo the greatest initiation that we have undergone together as a species, an initiation of fire that brings us humility and illumination. We will not transform ourselves and be worthy of this fabled earth if we aren't raised up in some way. The only way is to temper us with fire and with iron and with love.

I do not wish suffering on anyone. But the human race has failed in that solemn responsibility to fructify and enrich the earth, to add to her beauty, and evolve with her towards the fullest human possibilities.

We are not rising up to the greatness of the wonder woven in us.

We think we are only flesh and so our dreams are only of profit and dust. We think that there is no force anywhere capable of chastising us for our cruelties to the earth and to one another, our wars, our racism, our sexism, our injustices, our proliferation of poverty, our tormenting of the environment.

But there is a force which science does not understand. It is threaded into life itself, into the laws of physics and metaphysics. Some call it karma. I think of it as the natural tendency of the universe towards balance and harmony. This force is implicit in things. What we do will be done to us, the good and the bad.

We are receiving the fruits of the evils we have inflicted on you and on one another. It all comes back to us. Human emotion is irrelevant here, for it happens as a condition of reality itself.

This baffles science. It confounds those who see only with the eyes.

But we are in an age of catastrophes. We initiated the catastrophes. We will receive what we are worthy of, receive it with lamentation and self-judgement.

Dear Earth, you inspire our dreams and our art. You feed our bodies and souls. You house our bones when we are gone. You are one of the terrestrial planets, made of the matter and magic of countless stars that have lent you their magnificence that you may gift it to us.

Dear Earth, look kindly upon the folly that is the human race. Teach us with your silent wisdom how to live again, how to be simple again, and how to rise to the greatness and sense of universal justice that is our divine inheritance.

Yours lovingly,
Ben Okri

Emergence

Emergence

The way I look at it, we are at a point of emergency. Now the interesting thing with the word 'emergency' is that emergency means 'a state of emergence', so it's not necessarily something to fear, but it's a moment in time when we can actually turn things around and something new can come into being. And when you look at it, ninety-three people in the world, that's it. They happen to be heads of state, but they're just people. They hold the balance of what happens to our planet in their hands. They hold the outcome for people and planet, those ninety-three people. That's nothing. We can make that happen, I see no reason why not.

Polly Higgins

We Are in the Underworld

The real horn being blown at this moment is one some of us simply cannot hear. Oh, we see – the endless television clips of crashing icebergs, emaciated polar bears, and a hand-wringing David Attenborough – but I don't think we necessarily hear.

Climate change isn't a case to be made, it's a sound to be heard.

It's really hearing something that brings the consequence with it – '*I hear you.*' We know that sensation, when it happens the whole world deepens. If we really heard what is happening around us it's possible some of it may stop. From a mythic perspective, seeing is often a form of identifying, but hearing is the locating of a much more personal message. Hearing creates growing, uncomfortable discernment. Things get accountable.

I worry I have been looking but not hearing.

In ancient Greece, if you needed wisdom greater than human you went to the market square of Pharae in Achaea and created libations for Hermes, god of communication, messages, storytelling. There stood a statue of the bearded god. After burning incense, lighting the oil lamp, and leaving coin on the right of the deity, you whispered your question in its ear. Once complete, you swiftly turned and left the sacred area with your hands over your ears. Once out, you removed your hands, and the very first words you heard were Hermes speaking back to you. You curated these insights into your heart, pondered and then acted on them.

Isn't it interesting that the enquirer to Hermes kept their ears blocked till they were out of the market square, so as not to be assailed by idle, above-world chatter and think it divine? I wonder if we may be asking the question to Hermes but removing our hands too early.

I think we are in the Underworld and haven't figured it out yet. Both inside and outside us.

The strange thing about the Underworld is that it can look an awful lot like this one.

I recently saw a mist suddenly descend on my garden, it just rolled in out of nowhere. Very quickly all appeared different: no shrubs, no apple trees, it was a foreign landscape. The dead felt usefully closer, the silence deeper. In just a moment, the Underworld seemed present, as an atmosphere rather than concept, a tangible, seasonal shift not a distant idea.

This world can be Otherworld, Underworld, heavenly, hellish and all points in between. It can still be Arcadia, Camelot, Eden almost. That's why it's confusing. We still get to go on holiday, drink wine, watch beautiful sunsets. We still pay insurance and kids still go to college. But there is something happening. An unravelling. A collapsing, both tacit and immense in scale.

And into that fraught zone drifts quite naturally the Underworld. This is not the dayworld, this is the nightworld we are entering. It's not a mistake or aberration, it is fitting with the times.

But we are still using dayworld words. This is why so little works.

When we move into Underworld time, mythically the first thing to go is often the lights. This is a shadowed or even pitch-black zone of encounter. Nothing is how it seems on the surface of things. We have to get good with our ears. So to repeat, our eyes alert us to the wider situation, but it's our ears that alert us to the personal, the particular, the micro in the macro. This tends to be when the heart is alerted.

And there's just more of the Underworld about. Its tactile, tangible attributes. We have *Penthos* (Grief), *Curae* (Anxiety) and *Phobus* (Fear), those gatekeepers of the place roving ever more readily among us. Either chronic or acute, acknowledged or not, they are present at our table. So what happens when the underneath, the chthonic, the shadowed material starts to become more and more visible in our lives?

We start to fess up.

The Underworld is a place where we admit our red right hand. We give up the apotropaic.

An apotropaic act is when you ritually ward off evil. When you claim innocence unduly you are attempting a similar, unseemly act. Keeping your hands clean. So we could entertain our own hypocrisies for a while. That would be suitably sobering. When we start to remove the scaffold of smoke and mirrors propping up our lives, what is left? That is part of an Underworld etiquette.

I also have to say something deeply unfashionable: it is not relentless self-absorption that makes us realise our interior mess is directly mirrored outside ourselves. That's not vanity, that's attention. It's not hubris, it's horrifying clarity. If we don't attend to our soul's vitality with intent, then suppressed they'll run us ragged. They are not above catastrophe to get our attention.

Soul seems more dangerous to talk about than sex, violence, death or money these days.

As many nerve endings as there are in a body, are the messages attempting to issue forth between place, animal and person in regard to climate change. I think we should forget the rest and attend to ours. Staggering spiritual repair is called for. It is not just those bad white men in power who did this. We all did.

I believe something will crawl back out of the Underworld. It always does. But it may not be us.

The Underworld chews up soundbites, gnaws on the feeble marrow of platitude, pummels certainty or sweeping predictions into the greasy darkness of the cave to gobble later.

The Underworld speaks out of both sides of its mouth.

So being that's where I think we are, I suggest we should develop a little etiquette. Hold a little paradox, to speak out of both sides of our mouths.

I'm going to ask us to hold two seemingly contrary positions at the same time. That we could deepen into both.

1. Stop Saying That the Earth Is Doomed

You may be doomed, I may be doomed, the earth not so much.

And anyway, do you have any idea how offensive that is to the gods? To any amount of offended magics? Especially to your children? To the perpetual and ongoing miraculous? In the Underworld, such grand protestations reveal a lack of subtlety. Even hubris.

131

Who are we, with our unique divinatory access, that we seem to have information withheld from everything else in all time and space? And now, *now* we are suddenly cleaving to the 'facts' of the matter? Facts have no grease to the wheel, they are often moribund, awkward clumps of information that can actually conceal truth, not promote it.

I'm not even asking for hope or despair, I'm suggesting responsiveness to wonder. To entertain possibility. And to deepen. Cut out the titillation of extinction unless we really are prepared to be appropriately stupefied with loss. To stop trafficking in it just to mainline a little temporary deep feeling into our veins as we post the latest Ted Talk on social media. It doesn't mean it's not true, doesn't mean that rivers, deserts and ice floes don't daily communicate their flogged and exhausted missive, but there's an odd twisted eroticism, a western Thanatos that always comes with excessive privilege. And let's be clear, most of us reading this are excessively privileged. That it-all-will-end assists some poignancy to a life deprived of useful hardships. Not ever knowing appropriate sacrifice is not a victory, it's a sedative.

But when we prematurely claim doom we have walked out of the movie fifteen minutes early, and we posit dominion over the miraculous. We could weave our grief to something more powerful than that. Possibility.

Let the buck stop with you. Where is your self-esteem if you claim the world is doomed with you still kicking in it? How can that be? What are you, chopped liver? Is that *really* your last word on that matter? I'm not suggesting a Hercules complex land on your shoulders, but if ever you longed for a call to action this is the moment. And, at the very same time:

2. Approaching the Truth That Things End

Dancing on the very same spear tip, we accept our very human response to things ending. We don't like it. We loathe it. The good stuff at least. Though it is a historical inevitability, a biological place-holder, could we start to explore the thought that earth may appropriately proceed without us? Without our frantically curated shape? Could our footprints become pollen that swirl up for a moment and then are gone? I'm not suggesting we are anything but pulverised with sorrow with the realisation, and our part in its hastening, but I persist.

I'm offering no spiritual platitudes, no lofty overview, but for once we stop our wrestle with god and feel deeply into the wreckage of appropriate endings.

That even, or especially such catastrophic loss requires the most exquisite display for the love we did not know how deeply we loved till we knew it was leaving.

I think even to operate for a second in the Underworld without being annihilated we have to operate from both wonder and grief, at absolutely the same time. One does not cancel the other out, it is the very tension of the love-tangle that makes us, possibly, a true human being.

This terrible, noble counterweight is what we are getting taught. But it doesn't end there.

Something gets forged in that very contrariness: something that is neither-this-nor-that, a deepening, the blue feather in the magpie's tale, the Hermian move to excruciating brilliance through the torment of paradox, the leap of dark consciousness that we, in the name of culture, are being asked to make. The thunderbolt that simultaneously destroys and creates.

I once heard that to become a sovereign of Ireland you had to attach a chariot to two wild horses. One would lurch one way, one the other. You revealed your spiritual maturity and general readiness for the task by so harnessing the tension of both that a third way forward revealed itself. The holy strain of both impulses created the royal road to Tara. A road that a culture could process down. I'm talking about something like that. That's Underworld character.

Such sovereigns were not defined by what they ransacked, what they conquered, but how they regulated their desire, how they attended to the woes and ambitions of their steeds for a third way to reveal itself. Under great pressure and with immense skill.

The nightworld is where we are.

I say it. I say it till we may hear it.

And in that darkness, we remember what we love the most.

That itself is the candle.

Dr Martin Shaw

The Hospital

We are building a hospital, a place of refuge, a sanctum

We have been skilling ourselves for all that this time demands of us

We have been sending smoke signals to the future people asking them for advice on how to be good ancestors

We are building the walls from something our grandmothers said, from something our parents forgot, from something we picked up from a story about hunter-gatherers in a *National Geographic* magazine

The roof is a piece of my grandfather's house that I kept in a little tin on my windowsill

This place must be safe and dry

It must withstand the storm

We made the blankets from moss and grass collected from the rocks by the river that we remembered to love

Our mother is coming soon and we must be sure we have the medicines she will need

Tinctures for courage and a poultice soaked in drawing ointment for the new world order

We have been training ourselves as midwives, constructing the curriculum from the plants that come to us in our dreams, tracts from an old textbook on natural childbirth and a battered copy of *Indaba, My Children*

She is near now

Heavy with birth and blood and body

None of us know what she will birth

But we have been dreaming of this time

A squalling storm, a raging owl, a flaming frangipani, eight eagles

We have been making plans

A pantry of forest and topsoil

A larder of carbon

Stockpiling mycelium and relations rather than guns and baked beans

Growing food forests in our high-rise apartments

Accruing libraries under our fingernails

Storing in the pages of our skin the recipes for compost, for happy bees, for the cycles of sycamore trees

Vested in our bones, the way our grandmother made soap from the sheep fat she scraped from our plates after dinner

We are calling our great-grandmothers via the hornbill and hoopoe to remind us of the rituals for the afterbirth, for cleansing the bodies of our dead with oils and seeds, for how to make the sublime tears of wonder

We are singing the songs that remind our grandfathers to remind us how to restore the river and the primordial forest

She enters the apocalypse apothecary holding her belly, covered in blood and mud

She is supported on either side by the hackers and conscientious objectors, who heralded the breaking of her waters. They have been training for this day

Janus, keeper of transitions, endings and beginnings, awaits at the door, with a perlemoen shell and a smouldering bushel of mphepho

As she enters everything crashes behind her, the buildings crumble as the seas take back everything they momentarily offered up. Blood runs down the streets. The drought and the mud slide collide

A tide of black oil laps at the door.

Claire Rousell

Trusting the Spiral

Active Hope is not wishful thinking.
Active Hope is not waiting to be rescued
by the Lone Ranger or by some saviour.
Active Hope is waking up to the beauty of life
on whose behalf we can act.
We belong to this world.
The web of life is calling us forth at this time.
We've come a long way and we are here to play our part.
With Active Hope we realise that there are adventures
in store,
strengths to discover, and comrades to link arms with.
Active Hope is a readiness to engage.
Active Hope is a readiness to discover the strengths
in ourselves and in others;
a readiness to discover the reasons for hope
and the occasions for love.
A readiness to discover the size and strength of our
hearts,
our quickness of mind, our steadiness of purpose,
our own authority, our love for life,
the liveliness of our curiosity,
the unsuspected deep well of patience and diligence,
the keenness of our senses, and our capacity to lead.
None of these can be discovered in an armchair or
without risk.

Joanna Macy

Hope

A Scientist's Dream

From time to time I do think about the future. My dream is that the picture we so frequently paint will be different. Not the catastrophe that is so frequently forecast. But a world where the pressing problems are cut off, circumvented with human ingenuity and self-realisation and mobilised collaborative effort.

A world where humans decide the future to be a sustainable and transformed one that successfully reconciles climate change and our needs for food, energy and all of life.

That is what I imagine we can achieve.

Nathan Bindoff
Professor of Physical Oceanography
University of Tasmania

The Hawthorn Tree

Dear Precious Earth,

I'm eating mud. It tastes good. A worm slides through my small hands.

Lying on my back the grass is warm and smells sweet. Blossoming clouds move across the blue sky, changing shape as they go. Poplar trees sway in the wind. There is one near the house – reaching up to brush the sky with its leaves.

I'm on my stomach by the edge of the pond. Frogspawn is floating on the water. Black dots in jelly. The dots grow bigger. They break from their jelly and swim around. Soon they grow small legs and the tails drop off.

Butterflies crowd around the long mauve flower heads of the buddleia bush. They are excited. Touching and moving away, touching and moving away.

Age eight I climb the beech tree in Chipperfield Woods. I'm good at climbing, my arms are strong and I'm not afraid. I want to get to the top.

I'm in Connemara by the Atlantic Ocean, which is huge and full of jellyfish and seaweed. I swim across the mouth of a river, the fronds wrap around my legs. I'm not scared.

The earth weaves itself through my mind, memory and body. I'm part of the mud, the grass, the clouds, the sea, the river.

Now I plant wildflowers and a hawthorn tree; let the grass grow long. I campaign with my friends to transform the world, away from fossil fuels, away from greed, away from capitalism,

so that my goddaughter, Eleanor, and all young people and all
other life will have a future with you.

With love,
Emma Cameron

Corrections

Deforestation
It is a plague on every generation
Our nation doesn't care
Sending our forests up in flames
With it our hope salvation
Our children and our children's children living and
dying
In this hell we created
Flames are burning us alive
We started cooking without instruction
Now we are too close to self-destruction
Never knew what danger it would bring
We didn't know what it cost
Endless frustration
Just for what they call 'innovation'
They call it progress
They call it improvements
They say they are making break-throughs
In tech media and mental health
They say they care that they can help
Yeah let's go green they say
They try to create, to make, to attempt to help
But they have already done too much
Retrace our steps
Correct our errors before they become our mistakes
We are a ticking time bomb of our own creation

Only twelve years
Make **your** difference
Make **your** change
There **IS** still hope

Alex Morrison Hoare, 13

Thirteen

Dear Little Sister,

Today I will walk out of school, with the thousands in my city, millions in the world, and shout out and stand up for the future of our planet. For the change of the powerful and greedy. For the seas and her creatures who have died from our plastic nooses. For the land and her magnificent grey beasts and regal cats who die from our lethal greed.

I will wonder when you turn thirteen, twelve years from now what you will see: Have the people given up? Is our planet dying? Is the air we breathe as toxic and vile as cigarette smoke? The rainforests no longer lush and enchanting but broken and burned? The weather violently protesting to the poison we have fed it.

We have the answers, the solution and the methods. The scientists found them, the children cry them, and the politicians ignore them.

Tia Khodabocus, 15

Active Hope

I am not going to let you die. I am not going to let it happen. How is it possible, that you, who holds us all, who gives us the ground on which we walk, and the air that we breathe, are dying?

How can I wrap my head around this? I am so worried about you, I wake up in the middle of the night. Sometimes my face and hair are wet. It's just a scary dream I tell my children when they wake from a nightmare. But this is not a dream. It is really happening. I have that David Bowie song 'Five Years' going round in my head. I look at everything around me and often I just want to weep.

My children's future. This tiny fragile planet orbiting in space and we are all alone – all alone, how could we have let it come to this? Poisoned the earth, polluted the air we breathe, melted the ice caps. A thousand horror movies are about to come crashing down on us – are already crashing down on us. Fires and floods as you lie weak and feverish and are shaken by tremors.

We must dream a better outcome. We must hope, because without hope there is nothing. Hope does not mean waiting passively for everything to somehow right itself. It won't. Active hope. We must change for you to recover. And when I cycle through my city, I have started imagining the streets empty of cars. The wide streets, tree-lined and beautiful, made fit again for walking and cycling, and breathing fresh air.

And when I look at the sky, I imagine it devoid of planes and helicopters. Just blue. And wide.

I look at the sea and imagine it clean. No more plastic bags floating through the depths, ending up in the stomach of a whale far out there, no more landfill buried in the earth.

We can be radical. We can make change happen. And what makes me hopeful is that all we need to do is love you better. Care more. Teach our children to sleep under the stars, to love the birds in the woods, the sand under our feet. We need to change our aspirations. Don't say, 'That's nice, is that new?' Buying new should become socially unacceptable. We have all we need. Stop buying clothes we don't need. Stop buying plastic toys and gadgets. Stop driving everywhere. Change our habits. Become humble and careful with our resources. Teach our children to save water. Be grateful and be aware.

And take to the streets whenever you can, to make change happen from above as well. But don't wait for the government to sort it out either. We all need to make the little changes. And whenever you do, someone watching you will see. I love the man who refuses a plastic bag in the queue in front of me. I love the teacher who brings in a keepy-cup. I love anyone who makes a choice because they love you. We need to talk about it and we need to lead by example.

If we do all this, if we can dream a better future, we can take the first steps towards it. We love you fiercely, we all do – you are us, we are one. We just must not forget this, and you must now be our number one priority. Only then do we stand a chance. Only then do you stand a chance.

With love, and hope,
Tamara von Werthern

I'm Seeing Changes

I am all and everywhere that is dark, watching to see you
Well for all time. You, a whelky eye, that cannot see itself,
Blinking blue as the night lid lifts and drops.
Your silent guardian for many blinking days,
I need to tell you. You, the tall-walkers, word-talkers,
I'm seeing changes,
I'm seeing changes.
I've known the ways clouds curl over miracle green,
A cat's cradle of life held up by your forest fingers,
A time-woven mesh of water, soil, plant and flesh,
A gifting between bodies, within and beyond sight,
Invisible breathing, constant slow growing.
I'm seeing changes,
I'm seeing changes.
This. All this, is fraying as you chop the high fingers,
The weft is going and soon too will the warp.
You talkers, tall-walkers, you ARE earth!
But hammocked in that life-cradle you do not know
How you are part of it, how you are served, how you will fall.
I tell you, I'm seeing changes,
I'm seeing changes.
The ice that has cupped you, held you steady
Two white hands top and bottom, is less. Is less.
You, blue eye, have cataracts, vast eddies, ripping
Those forests faster than your machines ever can.
Plumes, feathery words, say Burn, Burn across the green.

I tell you I'm seeing changes,
I'm seeing changes.
And I tell you, you know it yourselves.
You feel the falling, the weaker cradling,
Even if you are not of those drowning or fleeing.
Be truth-talkers, tell each other of the falling you feel
Be tall-walkers, carry this truth and mend your home.

Bridget McKenzie

Sleeping in the Forest

I thought the earth
remembered me, she
took me back so tenderly, arranging
her dark skirts, her pockets
full of lichens and seeds. I slept
as never before, a stone
on the river bed, nothing
between me and the white fire of the stars
but my thoughts, and they floated
light as moths among the branches
of the perfect trees. All night
I heard the small kingdoms breathing
around me, the insects, and the birds
who do their work in the darkness. All night
I rose and fell, as if in water, grappling
with a luminous doom. By morning
I had vanished at least a dozen times
into something better.

Mary Oliver

Hope in the Darkness

The poet Mary Oliver died this year. Her poems have always summed up, for me, the relationship we can, and should, have with the natural world – the wonder, the peace, the beauty, the challenge of recognising how interconnected we are and must be with every layer of our planet.

I live in a beautiful, rural area of Hong Kong. Every morning I wake up to the chirping of the birds; when I walk home in the evening, the bats dart above my head and the frogs croak in a deafening symphony. There are water buffalo in the fields, red crabs in the wetlands and pink dolphins in the sea.

And there is also plastic, floating in the water, washed up on the shore, buried in the sand. There is an invisible layer of pollution choking the air and my lungs. There is the threat of the next typhoon, promising to flood rivers, break windows, and uproot trees. There is the news, every day, of another devastating environmental disaster, in Afghanistan, in Mozambique, in Australia.

The balance that Mary Oliver describes so beautifully has gone and every day it breaks my heart. Sometimes I feel suffocated by grief, inaction swallowing my desire for action, my attempts to share my fears with others collapsing in the face of what feels like our universal refusal, or inability, to truly confront what we have done to our planet.

But sometimes, now, I also feel hope. Hope that, if we can come together, we may still be able to save those 'small kingdoms [...] who do their work in the darkness', which Oliver describes so beautifully in her poem 'Sleeping in the Forest'. Hope that we may, again, remember the earth and be tender towards her as she has been to us. Hope that, together, there can be 'something better' for us all, to lift us out, finally, of this looming, 'luminous doom'.

Harriet Hulme

A Daring Invitation

As humans, at this awesome and terrible moment in our history, as we reflect on the greatest irresponsibility ever, and reflect on *our* concomitant great responsibility, we have a number of key needs. We need to love one another as well as to love this beautiful home of ours. We need reason and we need science and we need to stay in touch with the facts; but above and beyond those we need to trust, to have faith, to believe in the possibility of ourselves as earthlings even when reason says there is no reasonable hope and no reasonable doubt about the fate that lies in store for us and our planetary home. If we do not wager, if we do not act as if there is a chance that we can save ourselves, if we refuse to take the risk of being *un*reasonable, to hold out hope against hope that we may be able to save ourselves, then certainly we will fail to save ourselves.

Faith makes possible what for reason alone is impossible.

Let's *dare to hope*. It is a difficult invitation to accept, especially when there is so little basis for optimism: for we are hurtling full-tilt towards a cliff, and not even slowing down. We are planning to make the long emergency that we are in worse for decades to come, when we ought to be taking seriously the fact that every bit of heat we generate by burning carbon traps in its turn *tens of thousands* of times more heat in our greenhouse-ing atmosphere, which it stays in for decades. That's why we are in such desperate trouble; the time-lags are pitted against us, we have as yet little wisdom in action to change direction; virtually all the evidence suggests we are heading for likely terminal collapse of many planetary ecosystems.

Yet it is precisely *now* that we need such daring invitations, in order to start to make possible what the cool rational mind considers absurd, hopeless.

Hope can and must spring eternal, from nothing but the bare possibility of itself; from the mere fact that it ain't over till it's over.

Dr Rupert Read,
Whose hope lies in the Extinction Rebellion

An Apology/A Prayer

We're sorry.
We are deeply sorry.
We apologise unreservedly, without reservation.

So we may have given the impression
Quite unintentionally
Given the distinct impression
That the planet was not finite
That the resources of this planet were somehow
Infinite

(Going over our previous communications we now realise
     this *idea*, shall we say *hope*
may have been implicit)

The thing is our models, well, they seem to have somehow
Deceived us.
And by implication
You.
Who in a way might be seen to be

Us.

And yes we may from the vantage of now, we could be said to
    have given
Insufficient
Attention

ATTENTION ATTENTION ATTENTION

And for this, now, we would like
And we are unanimous in this wish
We would like to offer

ATTENTION

OK, in our defence
By way of
Justification
The prospects for the
FOURTH INDUSTRIAL REVOLUTION
The prospects for
POST-CAPITALISM
The prospects for
FULLY AUTOMATED LUXURY COMMUNISM
Looked, and on one of the good days still look
Exciting

And perhaps we found ourselves so gripped by the narrative
    of
GLOBALLY ACCELERATED GROWTH
Or the

INTEGRATION OF THE SOUTHERN ECONOMIES
Or the advent of
NANO-TECHNOLOGY

(I mean you have to realise some of us were born in a period
      when we could use the words
'the future'
say them:
'the future'

Entirely without irony or dread)

Somehow our models seem not to factor in, well,
They tended to be predicated on
What's the phrase

Ceteris Parabus

ALL THINGS BEING EQUAL
ALL OTHER THINGS BEING EQUAL
THE STABLE BACKGROUND
A – BACKGROUND

And in retrospect our models might have benefited from a
      greater degree of
RISK ASSESSMENT
That is to say they might have been
FUTURE PROOFED

And in our defence there was always one last patch of snow
  to ski on
One last pristine beach detected almost by chance by, say, a
  drone
One day where all the signals of a season remained intact
One species still caught by means of a camera
Trap

But the model seemed always somehow to suggest
That nature was the obstacle not the objective
That some of us have moved from abject rural poverty
To vertical urban living in one generation
Which is hardly to be belittled

We are the people that have turned money into a heartbeat!
Swathed the world in the embrace of electro-magnetic waves!
Delivered on-demand television and live-stream
  pornography!
All of these gifts, all of them stem from the model!

And no one, at least no one sane or of sound mind or that we
  knew of
Ever
Ever
Noticed ANY shortcomings in the model
And seriously, we know all the intelligent, all the smart
  people, literally
All of them

And anyway who might have imagined, really, that the drone
     of winged insects
The presence of frankly irritating and peripheral forms of life
Might now prove so

Critical

ATTENTION ATTENTION ATTENTION

And for this oversight, for oversight is what it surely is
We now wish to express our
Deep sadness

With the proviso that for the time being at least
By which we mean today, possibly tomorrow, maybe the day
     after that

There is no model other than the model.

A Prayer

*This is a prayer to no gods or all gods or anyone listening or anyone
     out there*
A prayer for no one i.e. everyone

Even to pray requires some sort of hope in a listener

Oh well, here goes:

For everything at the edge of its range, we pray
For island populations in their last days, we pray
For the bird with its beak in a ring-pull, we pray
For the geology of gameboys and smartphones, we pray
For the idea of seasons, we pray
For weather that can be forecast, we pray
For a harvest for the world, we pray
For the low-lying villagers, we pray
For the yet to be born and the unborn and the newborn, we
    pray.

For a crying against the dying of the light, we pray
For a rebellion against extinction, we pray
For 2030, for 2050, for 2070, we pray
For my children's children, we pray

That they breathe air of the correct chemical composition
That they swim in shockingly cold seas
That they might wake to the surprise of snow

That Donald Trump might slip into a long yet painless coma
That Bolsonaro might vanish in a Lear jet somewhere over
    the rainforest
That Tony Abbott might choke on some coral
That Putin might fall into a Siberian sink-hole without
    bottom
We pray

That the background rate trumps the FTSE Index
That Brexit will become a bump in the road
That we will boast bullishly about our minimal carbon
    budgets
That cars will baffle children in museums of folly
That roads will become flower-rich meadows
Super-highways for the auroch
That border controls give way to planetary boundaries

We pray
This prayer as large as life itself
Knowing there is no intercessor
No deus ex machina waiting in the wings
With his latest geoengineering gizmo

Oh earth
Poor abused earth

Hear our prayer.

Steve Waters

I Believe in You

Dear Earth's Young People,

It has been an honour for us to walk on earth's sand at the beach, just so we can get a glimpse at the infinite ocean, and watch the glorious sun set and rise each day.

It has been an honour for us to walk up her mountains, hills, and travel by water, air, car, and walking.

Therefore, I ask you young people to encourage keeping her beautiful by respecting her, preserving her for years and generations to come.

One thing we can do for the people and planet is to grow a tree. I didn't see a difference between planting and growing until I saw a quote written by a Kenyan woman that said:

'Anybody can dig a hole and plant a tree. But make sure it survives. You have to nurture it, you have to water it, you have to keep at it until it becomes rooted so it can take care of itself. There are so many enemies of trees.'

You see the difference too? When we grow a 'lung of the planet', the air is purified and our people are given fresh strength.

Lastly, we can share with and teach other people the importance of preserving the planet.

If every person we know could take one small step towards being greener, the collective effort could be phenomenal.

I believe in you.

Yours sincerely,
Your friend, Molly Wingate, 16

Dear Earth,

I'm writing from the early spring of 2019 and wondering how you are in 2082, when my eldest grandchild will be the same age as I now am. At least, I hope he will be and that you are able to provide him (and his younger sister and cousin) with the support and joy you have given me.

I think that will all depend on the next few years as we have now reached the absolute crisis point after so many years of shilly-shallying around, despite the best efforts of so many people. And yet, I am probably more hopeful now than I have been for several years: the wall of obfuscation and denial that has been so strongly defended by the fossil fuel industry and their wealthy backers seems finally to be cracking open. Even with the massive funds that are used to sustain it, it can no longer deal with either the evidence or the anger that confronts it.

People all over the world are finding common cause and recognising the strength of their numbers. Children have with horror discovered how badly their elders have compromised their futures. And, finally, politicians are realising that they have to listen even if many still delude themselves that they can get away with platitudes rather than actual actions. But, now and in the nick of time, there seems to be a chance that we will do enough to enable you to continue to provide a home for the wonders we are so at risk of losing and for us. And, I hope, we humans will have learned for all time that we are part of nature and cannot exist outside it.

With love, hope and gratitude,
Bob Langton

We Already Know the Answers

If we seek the essence of what makes us human, what it is that really differentiates us from the animals, we will find that the answer lies in our self-reflective consciousness and our capacity for cumulative cultural evolution – essentially, our fine-tuned abilities to learn from each other. This is a result, not of our competitive nature, but actually of our capacity for cooperation and our evolved ability to understand each other. Without these abilities, *Homo sapiens* would not have made it this far.

It is not a matter of travelling backwards to some idyllic past – it is not possible to reverse the passage of time and why would we want to, given all that we can learn and all we have gained from what has passed. But we do need to question where we think we are going and whether we can sustain this trajectory without hurtling to our demise. We seek purpose and meaning in all things external to ourselves and neglect the true reality that we are actually all aware of. We don't have any other purpose, the purpose of life is life itself. Without life in all its forms we are utterly destitute.

If there is one thing we can be grateful for in the challenges that this age presents, it is that we already know the answers, we have been on this earth for a long time. Civilisation is built on great myths that can be difficult to disentangle, but at the heart of it is the mentality of control – the use of people for ends other than what we were truly put on this earth for. Each person can liberate themselves from this in their own minds and transformation will surely follow. When the myths can no longer be sustained, we will once again understand what is useful, what is beautiful and how we can create societies that nurture ourselves, rather than alienating them. The call of the earth is powerful, but it does not matter whether we listen or not – for it will keep on turning regardless.

Eva Geraghty

I'm Still So in Love with You

Dear Earth,

I'm still so in love with you. I'm still stunned into silence by the rolling hills, the endlessness of the ocean and the ever changing sky. The birds that come and go, the insects busy about their business, running the show. The trees, solid; lives spread out so much longer than our own. They've seen it all, they've seen us come and they'll probably see us go.

We didn't deserve you and all your careful intricacies. Humanity, the spanner in the works. I'll do anything to fix this, but there's only so far reusable coffee cups and vegan sausage rolls can get you. I am small, I need bigger people, with bigger power to invest their energy in something worthy for once. The most worthy cause, the greatest of goods.

I am lucky, I see all the good, I see how much there is worth fighting for. I can't imagine how anyone can sit on piles of money, casually ignoring the rising oceans, muddled seasons and marching children. I don't know how anything can be considered more important than protecting you. Without you, we are nothing. But earth, if we can't save ourselves, if it takes too long, if the paperwork is too arduous and the debates inconclusive, please look after yourself. I hope in our absence you heal; I hope the animals thrive and the water is clean and the forests grow wild. But let's not allow it to get to that point.

Earth, I'm still so in love with you, and I can't be the only one.

Kerala Irwin

A Great Non-Conformity

Dear Earth,

Having just returned to New York City after travelling by raft down your Colorado River through your Grand Canyon, a shock the city, this first day, after sixteen days on your river, deep in your Grand Canyon, 2 billion years before today ... another great non-conformity.

I stand back while I stand forward. I eddy while I rush down river observing my need to take part, to be heard, to express my views, to obtain, to be needed, why, what need?

I stand also between forward and back, balanced on a paved walk, that is itself balanced on granite, deep dark quartz-ingrained granite, that is itself moving between then and now and all of us, every cell, bound to and born from this waltzing inner and outer core of molten compressed star dust.

I stand and collapse the high skyscrapers. I haystack, boil and whale rock them down into the avenues and side streets. The dam is dismantled, and I let my imagination empty out.

Fifty thousand cubic feet per second, more, roars down the avenues and swells into the numbered brutal grid. Debris begins to slide in from the cross streets and the yellow taxis climb and fall on rapid waves of my imagination over narrow gaps in the huge piles. Long rolling tongues swell uptown of these rapids and downtown flipped taxis cars and buses form submerged or visible jagged obstacles.

Times Square is a maelstrom and all the traffic heads one way, down town to the ocean.

I see the city collapse completely and the sea rise and flush it all out, concrete foundations, steel ambition, glassy vanity, brownstone, penthouse, office floor, all reduced to a layer of sediment, no, only a slightly different shade in a much larger layer of sediment. A matter of subtle geological pigmentation in a dried beach. A few inches in a 500-foot-thick blanket of sandstone rolled across the older manahata granite and Hudson River basin buried most likely for ever unless revealed in time to come by some post-historic river, earthquake or shifting tectonic plate ... to what to whom what for why?

My beloved has her hand on my naked shoulder. 'You're all right. It's all right,' she whispers in the darkness as my eyes open momentarily amid the embracing waves of sockdolager, granite, crystal, the dreaded Lava Falls, rapids, like our present age, where each night in sleep Psyche rows me again down Pan's Grand Canyon.

I stand also now awake beneath forward and back, within the universal darkness. I see the city obscure the stars – my travelling companions down the Colorado. Cygnus, the Milky Way, Orion, the distant Andromeda – all obscured above the city's man-made canyons and up-lit cliffs of show-times-square. But I know their infinite space is there. I know they are there always. Older than our earth, our sun, but of the same nature, the same dust that pools in the hotel bath when I wash my clothes and fills the tiny wrinkled tributaries and lifeline canyons of my sunburned hand holding down this page while I scratch about and scribble in another great non-conformity.

Wish you were here.

Many blessings,
A Sometime Broadway Actor.
Mark Rylance

A Nightingale Sang in Berkeley Square

That certain night
The night we met
There was magic abroad in the air
There were angels marching through this town
And a nightingale sang in Berkeley Square

I may be right I may be wrong
But I'm perfectly willing to swear
That we can turn this world around
And make nightingales sing in Berkeley Square

That moon that lingered over London's skies
That April moon he knew why
He knew that we are acting out of love
The whole wide world seemed to recognise

How strong we are, like never before
We are here because we care
But those hazy crazy nights we met
And dreamed nightingales sang in Berkeley Square

Our onward steps may be harder yet
But we've hope like we never had dared
To give a voice
For what's now so rare
Like the nightingales here in Berkeley Square

And now we kiss and say goodnight
It was such a romantic affair
It was no dream
I know, we were there
We heard nightingales sing in Berkeley Square
Those nights spent under London stars
And nightingales sang in Berkeley Square

Sam Lee

Discontinuous Change

Dear Fellow Citizens,

Not of England, not of Europe, but of this planet.

Thank you, to those of you who have put your differences aside and united to combat the catastrophe we are facing. Thank you for spreading this word, this movement, this energy, to unite the global population in a movement of non-violent, loving urgency. The earth will be eternally grateful.

Thank you for telling the truth, although it makes us uncomfortable. Thank you for refusing to hide the gruesome facts. For inspiring the young generation to rise up and have their voices heard.

The terrifying stories, reports, photographs – *the ones that the media are continuously failing to show* – may be a little overwhelming. The truth is not a pretty sight. There is a lot of shame in what we, as a species, have done, and we need to keep this in mind. We must be careful not to let the guilt and sadness pull us into a vortex of anxiety that inhibits our productivity. An overload of depressing information can oftentimes burden us to a point where it is too much. Where we lose hope, and hope is what is most important in this situation. We need to be stable and healthy enough to be in a space that allows us to create a productive response to any negative climate news or statistics.

Sometimes we feel as though we are too small. As though we are not big or strong enough to have a real impact. We all feel this way sometimes. When you do, when the small child in you is saying, 'I need help with this! I can't do it! I give up!' consider phenomena such as discontinuous change. If you put a bottle of room-temperature water in the freezer, there is a continuous change in the temperature of the water as it cools. However, if the freezer had a transparent door and you could watch the process, you wouldn't see a change until the critical moment where the water changes state and freezes. This is the discontinuous change. The water was always in the process of freezing, but you can't tell until it has actually frozen. Of course, this is relevant with climate change, but it is also applicable to our efforts. Don't give up because you can't see an immediate change. Consider how water, which is so soft and supple, can break a strong glass bottle when it freezes; it can even break concrete and stone.

It is important that we develop a strategy here. Not just because we need to overcome climate change, but to deal with new problems in the future. Of course this is our priority now, as it should be, but if something new arises, and it probably will, our knowledge of how to bring about change and spread awareness will help us greatly.

Go forward from here with fire in your hearts, and bring about the change you wish to see in the world.

The earth will be eternally grateful.

Mairéad Godber

An Island Travelling South

Dear Luna,

You once posed a question I found difficult to answer. I approached it sideways with anxiety, knowing the many ways the adults of today, and those before them, have both gloriously succeeded and spectacularly failed the enterprise.

You asked, **If we were to create a new nation, how might we begin?**

I am thinking now of the Tunisian fruit vendor, Mohamed Bouazizi, who in 2010 demanded '*dignity before bread*' before igniting the fuel that would produce the Thermopylae of his generation.

I recall an entry the poet Vera Inber made in her diary in 1941, while Leningrad reeled from the monstrosities of war.

'I am moved,' Inber wrote, 'by the thought that while the bombs rain down on this besieged city, Shostakovich is writing a symphony ... And so, in all this horror, art is still alive. It shines and warms the heart.'

We dwell too much on the thunderclaps of history that we sometimes miss the minutiae of human agency, our oxygen, the things that define who we are and who we ought to be.

This much is true: listlessness is not unique to your generation just as restlessness did not begin nor end with mine. And this, too: it is normal to gain your bearings while losing your marbles.

I wonder what I can tell you that you don't already know.

I am aware that we are bound by common truths. The ecumenical joy of open windows and a pinch of salt. The grace of Gandhi, the Force and Jimi Hendrix. The gift of Bette Midler, Bonnie Raitt, Susan Sontag and Steve Sawyer.

We know the great sky as the heavens or a short stretch of atmosphere, and that it is blue or dark depending on the time of day. We know the sun nourishes living and that stars are immortal, because as Captain Alatriste tells us, life is long until it ends.

Meantime, seas rise and reclaim entire coastlines, fields wither or drown, and mountains fall in heaps on whole villages as monstrous things burn and dig and burn.

I wonder how we got here, this point where we can imagine the end of the world but not the end of the dictatorship of consumption and accumulation?

The eminent scientist Stephen Jay Gould wrote in 1994 that the word dinosaur should actually be 'a term of praise, not of opprobrium. They reigned for 100 million years and died through no fault of their own. [But] Homo sapiens is nowhere near a million years old and has limited prospects, entirely self-imposed, for extended geological longevity.'

We know Gould is right. We are aware of the great danger we face together but we seem intent on courting it.

And so our war is with ourselves – with the amber of our indifference and the obstinate refusal to recognise the annexation of who we are and who we ought to be.

A transcendence, then. A self-surpassing. An awareness of our place in what Barbara Kingsolver called 'the sovereignty of

179

the animate land that feeds us and shelters us'. A confrontation with the choice of whether we shall abide by life's ruins and live the sanctioned life – or face the moral reckoning of our age.

There is really only one investigation all along, wrote the novelist Michael Chabon, 'one search with a sole objective: a home, a world to call my own'.

We are not so different, you and me, not as distant from one another as the decades that separate us. We are both searching for continuities and the elusive reboot.

For all the days when outrage starts to feel like calendared indignation, for the sheer number of mistakes repeated so many times it makes you wonder if we as a species are ever capable of truly learning, there are days that reward us with renewable joy: when love rules, when wisdom wins, when humility prevails over the conceit of our certainties.

So think of an island, my dear Luna, an island travelling south, a landscape on the move where compassion is the currency and solidarity the only debt people owe one another, a house of memory built with hope.

If you can imagine such a nation, you should know that I live there. And so do you.

Love,
Tatay

Time Stands Still

Dear Earth,

These are difficult times. Yet I feel you, telling us:

> Look what I can do when you all slow down.
> Remember.
> Remember.
> You are a visitor.
> This life is but a moment.

There will be a time, soon, when we will kiss our friends and really look and see them. I don't know when ... but I feel that something good is going to happen. We don't know what or when but something good *is* going to happen.

Say it. Claim it. Whisper it under your breath. Hold it like something precious, press it into your chest.

Something good is going to happen.

Be brave. Be still. Be kind.

Listen.

Freya Mavor

Action

Ancestors

To Our Ancestors,
What have you done?
What are you doing to help?
What will our generation think of you?

Nivya Stephen, 12

The Future

Dear Mortals,
I know you are busy with your colourful lives;
You grow quickly bored
And detest moralising.
I have no wish to waste the little time that remains
On arguments and heated debates.
I wish I could entertain you
With some magnificent propositions and glorious jokes;
But the best I can do is this:
I haven't happened yet; but I will.
I am the future, but before I appear
Please
Close the scrolls of information,
Let the laptop
Sleep,
Sit still
And shut your eyes.
Listen
Things are going to change –
Don't open your eyes, not yet!
I'm not trying to frighten you.
Think of me not as a wish or a nightmare
But as a story you have to tell yourselves
Not with an ending
In which everyone lives happily ever after,
Or a B-movie apocalypse,

But maybe starting with the line
'To be continued ...'
And see what happens next.
Remember this:
I am not written in stone
But in time
So please don't shrug and say
What can we do,
It's too late, etc, etc, etc ...

Dear mortals,
You are such strange creatures
With your greed and your kindness,
And your hearts like broken toys.
You carry fear with you everywhere
Like a tiny god
In its box of shadows.
You love shopping and festivals
And good food.
You love to dance
In the enchantment of time
Like angels in a forest of mirrors.
Your lives are held
In the beautiful devices
Familiar in your hands.
And perhaps you lie to yourselves
Because you're afraid of me.
But always remember
We are in this together,

Face to face and eye to eye.
I hold you in my hands
As I am held in yours.
We are made for each other.
Now – open your eyes
And tell me what you see.

Nick Drake

Dear the Humans of the Earth,

No. Don't walk away. Keep on reading, seriously. And don't you laugh. Will you laugh when YOU find out that your family and friends have gone, when smog billows over your city, when your favourite animals' existence we take for granted now is pulled apart as easy as a dandelion? We are at a time where if we do something, we MIGHT just stop climate change. We have found ourselves at a decisive turning point. The world can't just sit here anxious about this. We have to act because we are the killers and we must unite. YOU have to spread the word. If you refuse you will be refusing the small chance we have left of saving not only our own lives, but all the nature that relies on the climate. YOU will be the killer. There is already too much evidence to refuse the fact that the earth is in a cataclysmic crisis. We have inflicted pain on ourselves and we have inflicted pain on the animals that make us who we are. We are slowly killing ourselves. Look at the facts. Look at them now. Due to the greenhouse effect that's wreaking the world of our fossil fuels we burn maliciously, sea levels are rising. Ice caps are melting. INNOCENT Arctic life is dwindling. Forest fires are scorching INNOCENT wildlife. Plastic is strangling INNOCENT turtles and dolphins. Would you care if you had destroyed your best friends' lives? Would you care if the creatures you most admire are confused, dying out by being choked by a plastic bag? The world needs to care.

But to truly care you have to do something about it.

In this time, in this life, you have to care. Would you care, or would you watch your animals die out, watch your paradise crumple because you were too idle to do ANYTHING about it? You need to speak up for our wrongdoings. They will never be fixed the way we are going. We are too stuck in our era of modern technology we don't look at what we left behind. We left behind a haven, and we are killing it. We are plaguing it. If you're scared of sharks, look at yourself. You are the one animals are scared by, and there's no denying.

You, you humans, you only have eyes for technology. You don't care about the things that are a part of us. You are blind right now, and you should feel ashamed. You don't. You will in thirty years, but by then it will be far too late. That's why our last chance is now. Come out of this having listened and cared and feeling ashamed. It is becoming a reality. We need to open our eyes to the world or it will close its eyes on us.

Yours sincerely,
Luke Jackson, 12

Galvanize

The time has come to
galvanize those heaving sighs, from
fraught days and spiritual malaise. From
miles and miles spent in supermarket aisles,
overwhelmed by choices to the point where we
lose our voices and so, silently, we
loosen our ties to life.

But oh my loves, what magic we could make! if
we galvanized, realized beyond fantasized futures, the
power of our presence.

Yes. The time has come, to
get together, to claim the prize
of a collective awakening. Get off
our arses, realize our vastness and
put it to work: Stopping the shopping and stepping out
in the streets, battlefronts, shop fronts, fields,
boardrooms, classrooms, living rooms ...

It's time to galvanize.
To alchemize a fullness of voice, a radical
choice, to speak up for what we know
to be true.

Toni Spencer

No One Is Exempt

So here we are in front of hundreds, fighting for what we believe in. I am lucky to live in a beautiful place on a beautiful planet and what hurts my heart is people demonstrating indifference. There can be no claiming any more that, 'one doesn't know'. There is enough information out there and the people who have the power to create change are purposefully ignoring it.

Every day we all cry out, and beg, and recently march, for people to care. I have not seen any demonstrations that enough people care. And they say that stems from seeing 'no evidence' of the planet dying for themselves. Even where I live, the weather has changed drastically. As someone who recently became an adult, I am able to use the phrase 'when I was younger', by which I mean ten years ago when it used to snow. Not one hundred years ago when you could buy lemon sherbet for a ha'penny.

I want you to fucking listen to us. We are the ones in education with the information and a future that we are trying to protect. *No one* is *exempt*. Anyone who has ever heard 'you don't matter' in your life, listen to me, now you do matter. Care about the environment and I will show you how much you matter in this world.

Someone wise once told me, do not try to change the minds of those with power, they do not listen and are never affected. She said to create change, go to the people. And that is what this is.

You tell us as children that we matter, so why don't you listen to us? Imagine knowing that through destroying billions of trees and leaving us with the dire consequences – you directly impact the young generations' mental health. As politicians and money-hungry people, you have fucked our planet and yourselves up, then left it to us as unasked-for inheritance. I get told *all the time*, you 'young bright minds' can fix it.

WE ARE TRYING. Let us get on with it.

Again I implore you to listen to those who know more than you. Do not be afraid because we are younger than you, do not be intimidated by age differences. Don't be afraid of social embarrassment. Join our movement and make better recycling choices and we will be your family. There are thousands of us. You won't be alone. Remember: courage. You are supported. We love you all.

Ashby Martin, 18

A Massive Pink Vagina in the Middle of Oxford Circus

Hello everybody.

I'm here speaking to you as a Rebel, as a mother, and more than anything as a lover of life on earth. I'm a co-founder of Extinction Rebellion. We decided to do this thing in my house in April last year, but many of my comments today are personal views.

There is something about the situation we're in that I hadn't faced even as an environmental activist of several years. Something about being stressed: some part of me wanted to bury my head in the sand; some part of me was just enjoying the nice weather we've been having in the UK. But if we are to move forward it's essential for us to face this squarely, to look into this abyss that humanity finds itself at.

Life on earth is dying.

One in four mammals are set to die, one in eight birds, a third of all amphibians, 70 per cent of the world's plants. They talk about the insect apocalypse, the 75 per cent decline in flying insect species. One in five British mammals are set to be extinct in a decade. A million species are at risk of extinction according to the recent IPBES 2019 report. Wildlife is being destroyed by habitat destruction, overhunting, pollution, invasion by alien species and also climate change. We've got other ecological pressures too: ocean acidification is to double by 2100; pollution of the air, soil and water from particulates, plastics and chemicals; water depletion from the countries that supply the bulk of our food.

But it's not just climate change: the ultimate cause, the authors say, is overpopulation, and, more than that, it's over-consumption, especially by the rich. The idea that we can keep having economic growth doesn't make any sense to me. We have to de-grow the economics of the west and in fairness allow the economies of other countries to grow.

Those with the least responsibility for this have suffered the most.

We haven't tackled the extractivism that we've imposed on countries in the Global South. We haven't tackled those injustices, and they are now coming home to our children – who are not protesting when they're leaving school: in my view they're begging for their future, they're begging for their lives.

So while mainstream science and mainstream bodies are very much sounding the alarms, they are still unfortunately conservative. The paper *What Lies Beneath* was about the understatement of existential climate risk. Essentially IPCC models don't include tipping points and feedback loops, and Professor Schellnhuber was led to say that 'climate change is now reaching the end game ... The issue is now the very survival of our civilisation'. Jem Bendell, whose paper on Deep Adaptation has been downloaded over 450,000 times, estimates that social collapse is coming, it's inevitable – and it's soon. Not everyone agrees with that but it's a viewpoint: that immense catastrophe and massive loss of life is very likely and that human extinction is possible.

David Wallace Wells makes clear in his book *Uninhabitable Earth* why this civilisation is finished. Because when economic growth falls by 1 per cent for every degree of warming – and we're saying that we're heading for at least 3 degrees and probably more – then you can see that economic collapse is on its way, probably triggered beforehand by food shortages. The academic term is 'breadbasket failure'. We already had Lithuania last year in a state of emergency due to crop production and Latvia called its harvest a natural disaster.

As people accept that we have an emergency we have two very clear choices.

Do we want more democracy or do we want less? Because this democracy is not working for us in my view, it is a fake democracy.

Well. We're in a technology conference. And one of the main things I want to say here is that this crisis is founded in ecology more than in physics – and I speak as a person with a background in molecular biophysics. The earth is alive, it is interconnected; your body is not a singular body. You have a kilogram of organisms living in your body that keeps you alive. If you can close down your left brain, as I did one time with plant medicine, your right brain will tell you what the reality is: that you are interconnected and at one with the universe; there are no boundaries. We live in a paradigm that sees an ascendancy of the left brain, that focuses on reductionism; the idea that carbon atoms are somehow the problem that we're facing. This paradigm we live in is about scarcity, separation and powerlessness. And while I think technology might have a role as we walk forwards, I think we need to really focus on the fact that this is an ecological crisis. You can be in this conference with all this technology getting a bit of a hard-on about it, but this is not going to solve this crisis.

There have been five other extinctions. This is the sixth one. They've all had carbon dioxide implicated. The Permian-Triassic Extinction was due to runaway climate change, which caused methane releases. And we're seeing the melting of the methane clathrates now. We know the mechanism that could see 97 per cent of all life on earth wiped out. A paper that doesn't actually look at biodiversity loss, just the climate threat, said there's a one in twenty chance of effects that are beyond 'catastrophic'. 'It's the equivalent to a one-in-twenty chance the plane you are about to board will crash ... We would never get on that plane with a one in twenty chance of it coming down but we are willing to send our children and our grandchildren on that plane,' the authors said (Xu and Ramanathan, PNAS).

This is a Banksy that appeared at Marble Arch.

Marble Arch was beautiful, and all the locations were beautiful. I hung out with people I'd never met, and we had the time of our lives talking and feeling really connected and empowered, and how abundant it felt to eat vegan food we'd knocked up in the middle of a road that was supposed to have traffic running through it. Who needs to fly to Ibiza and have a burger when you've had experiences like that?

So what does it mean to look at this truth? For me it meant a feeling of a dark night of the soul over many weeks of grief. I expect to die; I expect my children will die. But that all life on earth will die? How are we to live in these times, how are we to stand up and talk about business opportunities and business as usual? We have to tell each other the truth. In the way we say it in Extinction Rebellion: We're Fucked. We are fucked. Humanity is fucked. It's a disaster, folks, of biblical proportions. And we have to allow in that feeling of grief. This is a feminine piece for all of us – men and women and all other genders – to feel the grief. Because when you feel grief, you feel love, and when you feel love you can feel courage. And let's take courage in the fact that the solutions to this crisis, which are multiple, are about re-loving nature, re-wilding, re-generating, reducing what we do, being together. But in order to see these solutions come forward we need to rebel. And we've started that with the Extinction Rebellion.

Civil disobedience is essential right now. The social contract is broken. I'm not organising protest, I'm organising a rebellion against my government. In April we occupied five locations in London over eleven days. Over 1,000 people were arrested. There are about 130 XR groups across the UK, but they're springing up across the world, in 58 countries. We pulled up a massive pink vagina, a big boat, in the middle of Oxford Circus with the name of Berta Cáceres on it. She's an environmental activist who died fighting for her land. So if you think some of us are brave being arrested here in the UK, we're simply using the privilege we have here. Over 200 environmental activists die across the world each year.

I think the experience we want to have as Extinction Rebellion is about prefiguring the human-scale changes that are needed. We are facing a crisis. But we need to do this together. The soil, the oceans and plant life, the biodiversity – these are the carbon-sucking machines that I'm choosing.

So as Greta Thunberg says, 'You only talk about moving forwards with the same bad ideas that got us in this mess,' let's not go around wanking over technology solutions and talking about things that probably mean massive extraction of more resources and more ripping off of the Global South. That's a process that's looking like death by a thousand cuts. This is about the rising feminine, the reunification of all of us coming together, *coming* together. Enjoying ourselves. Acting as if the truth is real. So join the Rebellion is all I'm asking you to do. And let's all be lovers.

This is not our Mother Earth, this is our Lover Earth.

Thank you.

Dr Gail Bradbrook

Taken from an address to a Cog-Ex Technology Conference, London, June 2019

Put Your Head in the Sand

Put your head in the sand,
Put down your hand,
Watch it all burn.

Or

Stand up and shout,
Banish your doubt,
Voice your concern.

Hannah Palmer

Use Your Voice

Dear Parliamentarians,

I have been a nurse for forty years; I have worked for the last ten with people with dementia.

Dementia is no respecter of status, wealth, class or prestige.

I have nursed doctors, lorry drivers and paedophiles.

I accord them all the same human dignity and respect; I give them appropriate care regardless of who they are and how they have lived their lives.

I have learned to communicate with those whom dementia has robbed of their ability to speak coherently; I have learned to communicate with those who are mute, literally having no voice.

You have a voice, and you have the status and power to use your voices to represent those of us with none.

My five-month-old grandson does not yet have words; he communicates his joy at life in myriad ways.

He laughs, he squeals, his smile beams like a beacon on a stormy day.

His joy is palpable; he wants to experience life in all its beauty and richness.

But if climate change continues as predicted by the IPCC what will be his future?

And what of the future for your children and grandchildren?

Please, on behalf of all of those with no voice, use yours to bring change, so we may all have a future.

Yours faithfully,
Marian Greaves
RGN/Mother/Grandmother

Correspondence

Dear Humankind,

Your recent wave of correspondence threatened to overwhelm me. It came so thick and fast.

To cope with the volumes, my emergency triage categorised your communicators as follows:

Group 1: **Poor Lost Souls:** their screams and agonies were carried to me on tropical cyclones, tsunamis and on the rising smoke of raging forest fires. The cacophony of human anguish was as nothing alongside the sound of fear and pain from the wider biosphere: nothing to be done.

Excluding California, silence from my northern and western hemispheres.

Group 2: **Awaiting Catastrophe:** their prayers were lucid, nightmares foreboding, and fears pervasive. Mankind on the move. Human flow. Testimonies that moved even me: from Mexico; Pakistan; the Pacific Islands; and the Horn of Africa. Plumes of anxiety from 50 million people in Bangladesh, with nowhere to go, as villages are slowly inundated by seawater.

This is where my sympathy lies, but I am powerless to intervene.

Group 3: **Prescient Activists:** this was formal correspondence, often poetic, sometimes angry, but mostly sorry. Sorry for the hurt. Sorry for the degradation and destruction. Sorry for the plastic. Sorry for the insects. Inspirational calls to action. Positivity in the face of pending doom. All heartfelt and all authentic.

Almost all from my northern and western hemispheres.

But what to do? What to do? I have no choice in what I do.

As one of your ancestors put it: '*For every action, there is an equal and opposite reaction.*'

The formal correspondence has stopped now, but there is no end to the shrieking of poor lost souls. No end to the waves of anxiety from my southern and eastern land masses ... from those waiting innocents.

Nothing to be done.

Unless **you** have a different view?

Yours sincerely,
The earth

Dear White Climate Activists

Dear White Climate Activists,

The climate movement is at a pivotal moment in which to stop the climate crisis in its tracks. But if we are to be successful, we must first resolve some of the barriers that have stopped us making progress. There is a crucial need for you to recognise that climate change has never affected us all equally. For you, what was once a far-off threat is now happening in real time; but climate change has already had a disproportionate impact on marginalised communities and the Global South. The climate movement has traditionally treated the fight for social justice and the climate crisis as two separate conversations, calling for action on one and ignoring the other. While it's likely that you understand that the roots of the climate crisis can be traced back to Britain's colonial history, in practice little has been done to align climate activism with systematically deconstructing social injustice, racial prejudices, corporate power and privilege.

The movement so far has been largely devoid of the experiences of the marginalised and the results have been stark. The movement chronically lacks diversity and has regularly failed to connect the dots between human rights and a just transition. This has led to glaring errors and distractions: climate change is not simply caused by rising carbon emissions, and it will not be resolved by recycling, veganism or a net-zero target alone. In a world where we are seeing both global and UK political leadership lean towards nationalism and fascism, the movement risks reinforcing these narratives if you continue to remain silent on the rights of marginalised communities. You must recognise that the work that is needed is simply the tip of the iceberg and will go on long after we have passed the twelve-year timeframe in which we need to take action.

This becomes most apparent in the movement's failure to stand in solidarity with migrants and people of colour. The UK's policies are the reason that inhabitants of the Global South are the first to face floods, drought, poverty, hunger and poor health due to climate change. They are the ones forced to migrate to safer ground or pushed out of their own land by international corporations. And when climatic changes occur, not only are human lives put at risk, but communities grow discontent, inequality grows, and nationalist and xenophobic forces attempt to exploit fearful populations. We've seen the same pattern emerge in the UK where there has been a parallel increase in anti-migrant, xenophobic and racist narratives – particularly from those with disproportionate access to wealth. It is often those same voices, the ones who have profited hugely from the climate crisis, who demand that we close our borders to those who move while we continue to invest in destructive foreign policies. The climate movement has contributed by further silencing marginalised voices, rendering them invisible, instead of amplifying them.

As climate change makes land uninhabitable and access to resources becomes restricted, the movement of people across borders will only increase. The World Bank estimates that migration will soar by 2050 unless carbon emissions are curbed.

Bangladesh is one such country which suffers from the perfect storm of climate events, experiencing cyclones, floods, sea level rise and temperature increases. Weeks of torrential rain in 2017 displaced 300,000 people internally, destroyed 100,000 homes and agricultural farmland. Many of those displaced moved permanently to urban regions, in search of new jobs and protection from environmental devastation. Internal migration has only increased poverty, particularly in Dhaka, as resources have become restricted. Soon, those same migrants will be forced to migrate externally in search of safety, where they will come directly in contact with hard borders with simply nowhere else to go. But their story is not part of your main narrative on climate change and their voices have not been amplified.

You will never win this fight alone and nor should you try to – the fight for social justice and against the climate crisis are one and the same. It's high time that the communities already affected by climate change are put at the centre of this debate. Centring them in this debate will ensure that we are responding to the climate crisis with solutions that holistically challenge the social, economic and political structures that caused it. Any movement that doesn't empower these voices, and isn't inclusive, will fail to create the critical mass of people that is needed to ensure that our collective voice isn't ignored by political leaders.

It will also fail to resolve the climate crisis because it will simply recreate the same structural injustices. If the effects and causes of the climate crisis are deeply political, then the solution must be too. To achieve true climate justice, we must think outside the box and embody the principles of equality in both decision-making processes and within our policy solutions, focusing on the needs of people over corporate greed.

We already know what climate justice looks like, but we must begin to make progress together. The climate movement must encompass decolonisation and action that seeks to dismantle sexism, classism, racism and other structural oppressions. Decolonisation must include reparations and redistribution, from the sharing of renewable technology with those in the Global South to a new green economy. We should aim for equality between nations as well as within them, alongside the opening up of borders. The global right to healthcare, housing, food and water must not be a secondary priority but must be the core of our journey to justice.

And never forget what you can learn. People of colour, working-class communities, queer communities and other marginalised groups have long been fighting a system that is designed to make us feel a sense of loss, to crack down on our collective imagination, to make us feel that we no longer have a purpose, and which denies us the very hope that we need in order to dismantle it. Trust our experiences and our expertise, trust our vision, and most importantly, trust that new leadership will bring back the imagination needed to transform the way we tackle the climate crisis. We are the experts in staring down existential crises, in resilience, and in winning battles while the war rages on.

Minnie Rahman

From Broken to Breaking

Broken glass
Broken steel
Broken bones
Broken

Broken forests
Broken trees
Broken leaves
Broken

Broken rivers
Broken streams
Broken water
Broken

Broken sea
Broken ocean
Broken fish
Broken

Broken earth
Broken grass
Broken animals
Broken

Broken ethics
Broken politics
Broken governance
Broken

Broken body
Broken community
Broken heart
Broken

Breaking greed
Breaking poverty
Breaking status quo
Break it

Breaking deadlock
Breaking inaction
Breaking corruption
Break it

Breaking injustice
Breaking violence
Breaking inequality
Break it
to repair it

Tamara Ashley

Liveable

To Earth,

You only just became liveable for so many of us: lesbian, gay, bisexual and transgender people; people of colour; disabled people; people from all marginalised groups who have only just been able to live full and happy lives. I am so sorry that with all the space you've given us we haven't respected you back.

To People who Live on Earth,

Don't take our communities away, don't take our spaces away, the world is only just getting good for so many of us, sustain the earth so it can get even better.

Casper Taylor

A New Civilisation

Dear Life,

I was not aware, when I was born, that I was born onto a battle-field. I was not aware, as I learned to walk, that I was stomping over the habitats of many creatures. I was not aware, as my mother drove me to school, that we were riding roughshod over the unmarked graves of our fellow humans. I was not aware, as we flew around the world, that I was attacking my child's chances. I was not taught, when I went to school, that we all had been drafted, as unwilling and unwitting child soldiers, into an army of destruction. I didn't read, in any of my university books, that my civilisation of towering buildings, zooming machines and feasting on the meat of other creatures was waging a bitter war against the promise of a possible future.

But now, I know. I can see how we were fooled, tricked into believing that shiny sprawling suburbs and industrial zones and manure lagoons and mines and drilling rigs were our new habitat. I can see how we were blinded by fossil fuel barons and captains of industry into thinking that cars and planes could replace the earth under our feet, even the clean air that we breathe. I can see how a culture built on ownership and consumption was merely an excuse, a fig leaf for the rich and powerful to accumulate ever more profits and power, leaving destruction and destitution in their wake, and a forever blighted future.

I can see many others waking up to the reality we face, of this desperate moment in time. I see their grief, their horror, their determination, their fragile hope as they realise they are not alone, and that their actions and words still matter, will still make a difference. I see them look around, searching for ways their energy and voice can be of use, desperate to join in the struggle for a possible future.

So now, I know. I was born onto a battlefield, but in this battle I am not alone. With millions and millions of fellow humans, I am heeding the call of a different destiny. A destiny not of consumption, not of burning the past and harming the future: but a destiny built on action and activism, on collaboration and cooperation, a new civilisation centred on preserving life.

Every morning, I wake from nightmares of rising doom and harm. I am drawn to the work of the day by the beckoning of you all, companions in this irresistible and immense task, by the lure of the struggle against the forces of fossil destruction, by the promise of this new future in whose service we are called, by life itself.

Julia Steinberger
Professor of Social Ecology and Ecological Economics,
University of Leeds

The Sixth Mass Extinction

Dear British Government,

I am writing to express my concern about the climate and how it is changing. Since I am not old enough to vote, I feel that it is necessary that I remind you that you alone hold our fate and our future children's fate in your very hands and that this fate seems like a destructive one. This leaves us youths in the position of asking the important question:

Are *you* willing to do anything about it?

I had a dream that I could be a hero and save the world but as time has gone forward I have seen that it is not possible. This is because the hero always works alone and as we have experienced, I am not alone; over 1.5 million people joined the campaign against global warming, which clearly shows that the whole world is keen to take action and become the hero to save this planet.

The earth is called **mother** for a reason. All the damage we have created is enough for the earth to hate us, but she still gives us the food and water we need. The evidence of this damage is as strong as brick: more than 2,000 scientists contributing to the IPCC have made it clear that cuts of at least 50 per cent to 70 per cent in global greenhouse gas emissions are necessary to allow our climate to re-stabilise. Therefore, the government should be making every effort to reduce greenhouse gas emissions – now. If you take a step back and look at the damage already created, you would think there is nothing to stop it.

But there is. We already have the options, so why don't you start using them?

If later in life, the increase of global warming carries on, I can look back on these days and I will remember why and who looked the sixth mass extinction in the eyes and denied it was happening. I will remember that the generation before me were too involved in 'important issues' such as Brexit to care about what was really going on. In Van Gogh's words, 'Conscience is a man's compass,' and if you, the government, has a conscience, you will lead us in the right path of change and action. Please give us hope.

Yours sincerely,
Luca Chantler, 15

A Failure of Imagination

Dear Artists and Writers and Poets and Musicians,

I'm writing to ask if you will help us.

Will you help us protect this precious earth, to inspire us to believe that it's not too late to act, to show us that each and every one of us can make a difference, and to convince us that the system can still be changed?

I ask this of you because I recognise that politics has failed.

As a politician myself, that's not an easy thing to admit. But I know that even those politicians who understand the urgency of making the transition to a zero-carbon economy have not succeeded in persuading parliaments around the world to act with the speed and determination that's necessary.

In our obsession with policies and procedures and parts per million, we've appealed to the heads – but have failed to touch the hearts – of the people we represent.

Yet the overwhelming question we face today is one that needs not only an intellectual response, but an emotional one, too.

Why didn't we save ourselves when we had the chance?

Those words quite literally haunt me. I wake up in the night with them going over and over in my head. Ten simple words that are spoken by the late, great Pete Postlethwaite in the wonderful film, *The Age of Stupid*. He plays one of the few survivors of climate catastrophe in 2055. And as he looks back at reels of television footage, real footage from weather events from the past few years – the typhoons in the Philippines, the heatwaves in Australia, the freezing temperatures in the US, he poses this simple question – and the hairs go up on the back of my neck.

It's the most important question of our time.

Why is it that we seem to be content to be the species that spent all its time monitoring its own extinction and its wilful and knowing destruction of its own fragile and precious home, rather than taking active steps to avoid it?

Many reasons have been suggested. The power and vested interests of the fossil fuel companies, for example, who are increasingly not simply lobbying government, but being given senior roles within it.

Or that people are just too busy trying to get by: trying to cope with the latest obscenity from a government intent on making the poorest and most vulnerable pay the highest price for an economic crisis not of their making.

Or that we're being bombarded by thousands of advertisements each day, all of them persuading us to go out and consume more – to spend money we don't have on things we don't need to make impressions that don't last.

But more than any of these, I think, what stops us from acting is the fact that we rarely have the courage to *emotionally* connect with the reality of what we're doing to this one beautiful and precious earth.

Academically, theoretically, we know about the dangers of exceeding 1.5 degrees centigrade of warming – but one of the reasons we don't internalise the reality of that is that we fear the darkness that might engulf us if we do.

How do we cope with the thought that humanity might not wake up in time?

That climate change might become irreversible?

That societies, even in the developed world, might no longer have the ability to respond or cope?

How do young people in particular cope with the reality that their parents' generation has brought this earth close to collapse?

When we really connect and *feel* the reality of what we're doing, such feelings of powerlessness, of despair can be difficult to escape.

And that's why we need your help. We need you to paint the positive pictures of how the world *could* be – and to tell us the vivid and compelling stories that show us that, when people come together and act, there is *always* hope.

We need you to remind us that human beings are endlessly caring and creative and innovative – and that if we choose to, we can set our minds to anything.

We despair when we have no stories to describe the present and shape the future.

Political failure is, at root, a failure of imagination.

But with your help, we can rekindle our imaginations and rediscover the power to act.

Caroline Lucas MP

Waymarkers

One: You are the lifelong island: the lucid stillness of summer morning, deer tracks in the bracken, blackthorn on flesh. Tides, their waxing thrust of neap and spring; sea-wrack; salted timber smoking in the dusk. Crab guts laid open on innocent rocks. Brambles fattening. The ashes of my father in the wind.

Two: You are – to teenage eyes – the Brontë-inflected drama of the Peaks and Pennines, their brown carpets flung out under sombre skies.

Three: Scots pine, rowan, blaeberry. You are snow on juniper branches; the rhizomatic roots of aspen trees. You are pine marten scat; you are the ghosts of lynxes yet unborn on British uplands. *Allt Ruadh.* Under the skins of language, knowledge of the land.

Four: You are a great mossed mass of wet forest and ponga ferns beginning to steam in gathering sunlight. The curved flank of a bay, a tender lick of spit between the rippling grey waters in the rain. Another island: its sloping biscuit shingle, its flush of greens and of yellow gorse, and fat, glossy, purplish pigeons shocking from the branches. In the rearing sounds: sleep-shifting-deepening blue, and the dark tannic gurgle of the burn.

Five: You are the river water slipping cold about my body this bright spring afternoon. Its electric tingle.

Six: The hardest thing is to look beyond ourselves. To perceive the complex webs of interdependence in which we are entangled, and over which we must not have dominion, and then to accept and to celebrate them. Nurture them. For their own sake as much as for our own (nor are we separate).

Seven: The easiest thing: to plant a million trees that we ourselves will never see come to full fruition.

Eight: The poet Gerard Manley Hopkins, secret eco-conscience of the Victorian age: 'What would the world be, once bereft / Of wet and of wildness? Let them be left, / O let them be left, wildness and wet; / Long live the weeds and the wilderness yet.' Let us keep faith with him, and with the wilderness.

Megan Murray-Pepper

There Is No Excuse

I was born halfway through last century in a town in the middle of Buenos Aires province, Argentina.

When I was small you could clearly see the Milky Way from my street at night, in summer thousands of insects of all kinds scuttled over the pavements, flew over the roads and car windscreens used to get covered in the bugs that collided with them. There was an incredible diversity of flora and fauna and we couldn't imagine a world like today's, in serious danger of collapse and with the extinction of masses of species every day.

I refuse to leave a desolate world for my daughter and her children, if she has them, that is if the human race hasn't gone extinct.

We must fight to put the brakes on climate change.

This is an emergency and there is absolutely no excuse for ignoring it.

Silvia Rodriguez
Writing from Sitges, Cataluña, Spain

Johnny from Sainsbury's Checkout Begs

Dear Government (or whomever it may concern),

Please. I beg. She begs. He begs. Greg from work begs. Pat from school begs. Johnny from Sainsbury's checkout begs. We all beg. On behalf of our planet, we beg. You wouldn't smash up your television screen or destroy your furniture or wreck your grand piano. Just for your plastic bag or your crisp packet or your McDonald's straw. This means that you definitely wouldn't watch your world rapidly die and suffer under your watch. Just for your children. Your grandchildren. Your great-grandchildren and all the future generations to come. But you do. You don't care if in the future, children won't be able to swim in the sea or climb trees or even breathe without wearing a dreadful mask. You don't care if global warming is killing bears, fish, birds, lizards, insects, big cats, cattle, frogs. Humans. Humans die due to extreme weather conditions, landslides, floods and droughts. You just watch and announce that we need to stop climate change while you are in your mansion, stinking rich from deforestation and the mass production of plastic. People all over the world fight for our planet and the plants, animals and humans within it. But not enough people. Animals can't help with climate change. Animals can't stop driving cars which pollute the air. Animals can't stop launching rockets into the sky, wasting materials and sending junk into the atmosphere, and around it. Animals can't stop driving noisy speedboats and jet skis and cruise ships which send oil into our oceans and mess with whale calls. Even if they could, why should they? They didn't start this, we did. It's our responsibility to do something before it's too late and you need to make sure that happens. Stop fussing on tiny problems such as Brexit, start focusing on the more important things in life. That thing is life.

Lilli Hearsey, 11

Last Generation

Dear Humans,

I am thirteen. In April I will be fourteen. I never wanted to spend my day of celebration being depressed, knowing that species are being pushed to the brink of extinction on the day I was born, and it pains me to think that.

Some people blame the past, I say blame the now!

We are the ones wearing all the make-up that uses oil from huge farms that replaced the rainforest; we are the ones that eat all the fast-food-chain food that uses transportation that pollutes the air that we breathe.

But we are the last generation that can do something – still, no one from the government has helped us although we have asked them, but they reply with a 'speak to the hand cuz the face ain't listening'.

Love,
Trilby Rose, 13

Enterprise

As the climate changes
the finance we refused will seem small
it costs more to mend a body wrecked
than to break its fall

now that our body is falling,
flailing limbs of blue and juniper green
dropping
to the jaws of a hurricane,
the leg will suffer what the foot has done
and the arm, the hand
and the shoulder, the neck
the waters and land: a foreboded wreck

mitigation and money are sisters
together they'll nurse the world
mending the cracks
aligning the spine and
supporting the back
caring for the skin
as it meets with the skies
knowing where to begin
raising clean enterprise
like open palms that say
tomorrow will be better if
you prepare for it today

Rakaya Fetuga

After the Rebellion

Dear Earth,

I'm sorry that I shouted, I was worried and scared, exhausted and overwhelmed. I had been burying my head in the sand, not facing up to the truth, because it made me feel sad and angry. Because it is too big and I felt overwhelmed. I'm sorry I haven't given you the attention that you needed when you have been asking me to help. I should have been shouting at our government, at the corporations, at the money-makers and decision-makers.

I want to keep you safe, protect you from greedy men and selfish neo-liberalism. I want to tell you how amazing you are, beautiful and funny.

I want time to stand still for a little while. I mean the linear time of trains, factories and freight lorries. Let all the schedules halt, the deadlines for production freeze, inactive for a long moment.

While we look one another in the eye, my eyes, your sky. While we listen to the chaffinch in the beech tree at the foot of our mountain and I feel your breeze blow cold on my cheek.

Make them all stop debating in their nasal voices about economic growth. While we plant a forest garden in each community.

If we all breathe in at the same time and exhale our warmest, strongest lungful to blow down the inflatable statue of capitalism, we will have a moment while it is floored. Suddenly vast spaces appear that were occupied by that eyesore and in its place swarms of creativity populate and multiply – we breathe it in and out, exchange and cross-pollinate.

You and me, earth. I and millions and millions of humans have found ourselves awake and conscious, feeling love for ourselves, for one another, love for every living organism, love for our geology, love for the flowing water and composted earth.

We have felt the dawn creep through the curtains and gently warm our spiralling core. We know the time is now. This small crack, if we have the courage (and we do), this crack can be prised apart – right open. As if opening our hearts to the possibilities of life when homes, food and resources are shared equally among us and we live as we are, part of you, earth and you are part of us.

If what is left after the rebellion is the raw ingredients of life – our bodies, plants, animals, soil and water, we are then an organism again without hierarchy.

We are one organism, one body, one planet, one love.

This is the time to heal the disconnections. Repaint the trails that have been disrupted by the walls of oppression. Sew and mend the tears and rips made by greed.

We will do it together, with kindness, positivity and love.

I love you.

Eve Houston

Turning

Dear Earth,

No matter what we do, you will go on turning. As a planet, you will survive us, in timescales we cannot imagine. But our disrespect matters. It is a matter of life and death for every creature – including humankind.

We need to take responsibility for pain we cause, to any being in your living surface. We need to start at our source – with you. Our relationship should be part of every decision. Because only when we remember that humanity is inside and not above ecology, can we truly call for justice.

This is not a missive, but a mission. A battle cry against ignorance, arrogance and alienation. All earthlings are siblings, and we have the chance to act accordingly – to act kindly. So, I want to make a promise. Just as you turn to face the sun from every angle, I will turn to you for my truth. And I call on others to do the same.

With love,
Fiona Glen

The Time Is Now

The time is now. Not in the next five, ten, thirty years. Now. Time has been wasted doing nothing – people have known we need to change for years. Nothing has.

That's why we are standing up and making our voices heard. We are doing our homework, but the government is not. So, don't tell us to stay at school, because we are clearly educated enough to recognise that something needs to be done. This is an emergency. Stop fracking up our future, because you are not the ones who will have to live in it. There is no planet B! Brexit won't matter when our planet is dead. If we carry on as we are, that will be in twelve years.

With youth strikes taking place globally, the government are being forced to listen.

Today's government aren't behaving responsibly. If they were, something would have been done many decades ago. What makes me angry, is that nobody seems to care.

People in Africa are losing their homes to the rising sea level and dying of dehydration due to the dangerously high temperatures causing their lakes to evaporate.

However, it is not just in Europe and Africa. All over the world the rate of carbon emissions being released into the atmosphere is damaging our health and heating up our planet at a rate we cannot control.

The reality is harsh, but it's ours to sort out. We have the opportunity to make a change. It's for our future, and the future of our children, grandchildren and great-grandchildren, and for the future of our entire race.

Dulcie Deverell, 14, and Edi Rouse, 14

Samaúma

I am the Samaúma,* a giant from the Amazon.

I am considered a sacred myth by the native peoples of the forest.

I have the ability to charm those who cross by me, for my beauty, my magnitude. For my wisdom that conquers throughout my life. From high up I take care and protect the other trees and those who live in the forest. I am the tree of life, I am a stairway to heaven, I am the mother of all trees.

My huge roots store drinking water, I am also a vehicle of communication in the forest; by tapping on my lush roots, the echo extends over great distances, indicating the location of those who need help.

I am matriarch of a perfect ecosystem – I am the connection with the Amazon socio-biodiversity, and I am witness of the wonderful life created by God.

And I, bearing in me all these symbols – I make my cry, my lament and repudiation be heard.

I am shouting against the disrespect for my beloved forest, the lack of an eco-consciousness.

I am denouncing the greed, the desire for profit and the predatory extractivism that pollute, kill, suck and exploit the Amazon rainforest, steal our mineral wealth, cut down our trees, degrade and weaken our natural goods, exploit human

* Samaúma is a tropical tree native to various parts of Latin America and the Caribbean, including the Amazon forest.

life, exterminate native indigenous peoples, quilombolas, and riverside communities, rob our children and women, enslave our populations and decimate our animals.

I cry out with all my might, I want to make my voice heard, I want to communicate through the sound of my roots deep in the Amazon ground: no more exploitation, no more evil, no more mining settlements that invade indigenous territories and bring serious illness to our children, no more deaths, no more deforestation for monoculture or cattle-raising that destroys the forest biodiversity and causes devastating climate change. Enough of using progress as an excuse for the depredation of our way of life.

I cry and I lament, I mourn the pain of my Amazon. But I am wise, my wisdom comes from distant times, and I see hope spring up in the new generations, in the youth taking to the streets of our 'village-world'. I believe in environmental education for the preservation of LIFE, I believe that the care of biodiversity, of human rights, the awareness of co-responsibility, the respect for the religiosity of the peoples of my forest, the fight against intolerance and the promotion of peace can restore life to the planet and transform the present and future of this world.

Therefore, I, from the heart of the Amazon, call you to change your attitude, to respect the worldviews and traditions of the forest peoples, and to join forces in building justice and seeking actions that defend the future of our planet.

Samaúma from de Amazon

Written by Bishop Marinez Rosa dos Santos Bassotto, together with the Artisan Indigenous Women Association from the Alto Rio Negro

The Age of Restoration

Dear Earth,

As one mother to another, I want to apologise for the mess we humans have made. In just a few hundred years, we have burned down your forests, poisoned your waters, acidified the oceans, melted glaciers and ice caps, and managed to upset the delicate chemistry of the entire atmosphere.

But here is the good news. We've already worked out you are 4.6 billion years old, gone to the moon and Mars and sent messages deep into the universe to tell everyone about life on earth. Something magical is happening too. Millions of ordinary people, especially our children, are rebelling against the old ways of thinking. Ways that led humanity to death, destruction and the glorification of domination of nature.

We've finally understood that everything and everyone is connected. We've understood that ending domination of nature goes hand in hand with tackling all forms of domination and hierarchy. The struggle to honour you, our shared home, and to achieve ecological balance and justice goes hand in hand with achieving racial, gender, sexual and economic equality. These struggles are linked and the movements to achieve them need to join up and overturn the prevailing order.

That is actually quite a leap in understanding. It's happened because we have allowed our creative curiosity to see you, dear earth, and ourselves, with new eyes. To see your abundance and how it could be used to provide the needs of all and not the few. More power from the sun hits you, dear earth, in a single hour than humanity uses in an entire year! We are trying to figure out how to harness this through solar panels, so we no longer have to rely on digging up coal, gas and oil. Once we have this power, we can generate and store clear water, so no one has to face drought and famine ever again.

But we can't get to that point till all of us unleash our imaginations. Too many people are panicking and either looking to the past for solutions or see salvation only for the few. It's bizarre that it is easier for us to put a man on the moon than imagine a kinder, inclusive and more equitable global society here on earth.

I am certain that in the end those who are panicking or trapped in the past will not have the upper hand. There is hope in the millions rebelling all over the world. Our artists, indigenous peoples, wisdom-keepers from myriad lineages, young and old people everywhere are forging new alliances, networks and coalitions. They are figuring out how we can care for each other even if the benevolent life conditions you created for us get harsher. It's an exciting time to be alive. To witness the conscious co-creation of a new era of humanity.

Bear with us, dear earth. The age of restoration and respect is almost here.

Farhana Yamin

What We Do Now Matters

They are wanting to tell us something, the future people.

The people of whom we are the ancestors.

Yet they are the wiser.

They are wanting to tell us that what we do now matters.

They want us to know that they see the dismembered ways that we live and how difficult it is for us to remember how to return to the family of all things.

But their existence is testament to the fact that it is possible.

They know we feel trapped by this system of entanglements and obligations and the amputations of our imaginations in a system that only ever intended to keep us blind to the bars of our cages.

But they want to remind us that there was a time when we could not imagine a world order that was not based on the divine rights of kings.

And before that even, there was a time when we knew what it was to belong.

When we knew we were Eland, Mantis and Dancer.

When we knew we were the firefly and the ocean, the stuff of stars and the breath of birds.

They ask us, stroking our hair and touching our faces, how did you know that something else was possible? Where did that idea germinate inside you? Show us, point to the place.

Tell us the story of summoning your brothers and sisters to revolt for a life of connection and dignity. For what dignity is possible if dignity is not available for all?

They ask us, how did you manage to build this world in the flames of capitalism, and yet all the while you were disconnected from your rituals, from the rhythms and songs of your people, the tiny sacred acts of care that ensure that the world is recreated with every dawn chorus?

How did you handle knowing all that you knew without becoming paralysed with terror and despair?

What did you do with your despair, personal, collective, ancestral?

How did you carry its magnitude in your heart without being overcome with madness, or perhaps while carrying your madness, your addictions and your chronic sadness, never really knowing the full extent of your vitality?

Did you carry pieces of it everywhere you went, stuffed in pockets and purses like used tissues, pulling out every pot and pan as the house flooded with tears?

Did you feel it hanging in the air and walking alongside you, the ghosts of extinct creatures following you around reminding you of all that is at stake, suffocating you with the thickness of their memory?

Did you taste it in your food, forced from the soil and sea with chemicals and violence, food that no longer nourished but flared up in rashes and welts as it entered your body?

Did you feel the suffering as you dressed yourself in the forced labour of people and animals, their exhaustion stitched into the seams and hems of your clothes?

We see you, they say, standing on the shore with 500 years of industry and environmental wreckage and slavery and

237

torture at your back, gasping under its weight, with only the vast black sea in front of you.

We see you.

We see you holding the crumbling world in one hand and the germinating seed of life in the other.

We know you are listening. Listening to your children, to the wind, to the birds, to the voice that startles you from sleep just before dawn, to the harbingers of a new consciousness.

We feel how you allow your heart to be broken while every day preparing the house for love, making up her bed, setting a place for her at your table. All with no good reason for hope and every reason to despair.

We see what is to come for you. And what will remain when the storm, from which there will be no refuge, is over.

We see in you the thousands of varieties of potato and corn and wheat, the cornucopia of culture and craft, language and art, the compassion and commitment to the value of the life of the individual and the group. We know what you have known across time and species, across geography and incarnation. We know what you are capable of.

We salute you.

Because what you do now matters.

Claire Rousell

Sea Change

You may think that you are simply one small positive
droplet in an ocean of troubles. A droplet that can't do
anything. But if you search our ever expanding ocean
you will find millions of other small droplets with the
same mindset as yourself. Together you form a sea in
an ocean. That sea can stir a storm. That sea can
make a change.

Harkiran S. S. Dhingra, 15

The Time for Action is Now

This was the last line of our callout for letters back in the spring of 2019.

What we had invited was more than just a call to act.

It was a call to sit with and process the times we are in.

It invited people to take a moment, to switch off the noise of daily distraction and horror, from business as usual, and to write a letter responding to this crisis.

These letters document what it is to be alive in the midst of climate and ecological breakdown. They may have been written by individual hands, in singular corners of the world, but what they attest to is the fact that we are not alone. We are deeply connected.

Letters to the Earth is an ongoing campaign, and one part of a much wider and unstoppable movement which includes some of the voices you've read in this anthology: Dr Gail Bradbrook, co-founder of Extinction Rebellion; Blythe Pepino, co-founder of BirthStrike; Daniela Torres Perez, co-founder of UK Student Climate Network; Bridget McKenzie, co-founder of Culture Declares Emergency; Sam Lee, co-founder of Music Declares Emergency; Jem Bendell, founder of Deep Adaptation Forum and Polly Higgins, founder of Stop Ecocide.

Get involved. We need to rethink and reimagine what was previously deemed impossible.

The stakes couldn't be greater.

The time for action is now.

Share these words and keep writing your own.
Speak them, hear them; make your voices heard.

We encourage you to:

Write

Your own letter to the earth, to think beyond the human narrative and bear witness to the scale of this crisis. What matters to you? What change do you want to see?

Organise

A letter-writing or reading event – in your workplace, school or community.

Share

Your words. Read your letter out in groups, in community spaces, in protest. Share it on social media using #letterstotheearth @culturedeclares

In writing and sharing these letters with others, new conversations and new possibilities can emerge.

Let this book be something you can fall back onto, whenever you need to tap into larger sources of resilience and inspiration.

As the environmental activist Joanna Macy says (so well), '*active hope is not wishful thinking*', it is a practice.

It requires playing an active role in bringing about change.

Find and play your part.

For further information and resources about the
Letters to the Earth campaign:

www.letterstotheearth.com

T: @culturedeclares
I: @culturedeclares

Creation
is the antidote
to despair

Acknowledgements

We are grateful to all the contributors, for their generosity and trust.

We would also like to express our thanks to the estate of Polly Higgins for giving permission to include her writing posthumously.

Thanks to the following people and groups who helped bring *Letters to the Earth* to life, both as a campaign and as a collection.

Ruth Ben-Tovim

Bunker Theatre

Alanna Byrne

Tom Cagnoni

Jack Chalmers

Christian Aid

Lucy Davies

Dan de la Motte

Stephen Dillane

Paapa Essiedu

Vicky Featherstone

Jack Gamble

Lorna Greenwood

Alice Haworth-Booth

Molly Hughes

Lizzie Jackson

Maya Kirtley

Sam Knights

David Lan

Alex Lawther

Jennifer Lim

Chirag Lobo

David Luke

Alice Malin

Freya Mavor

Ellen McDougall

Ronan McNern

Jackie Morris

Jane Morton

Andrew Medhurst

National Theatre Studio

Lucy Neal

Edward Nelson
Ben Okri
Tamsin Omond
Tamaryn Payne
David Ralph
Lee Ross
Sarah Rowe
Justice Savage
Andrew Scott
Hannah Scott
Shakespeare's Globe
Irene Sinou

Jack Smyth
Chris Sonnex
Oscar Stephens
Simon Stephens
Emma Thompson
Naomi Wirthner
Caroline Wood
Jessica Woollard
Margita Yankova
The 52 venues who took
    part in the 12 April 2019
    action

Quotation

Essay

Image